THE POWER OF POETRY

Scotland

Edited by Donna Samworth

First published in Great Britain in 2013 by:
YoungWriters
Remus House
Coltsfoot Drive
Peterborough
PE2 9BF
Telephone: 01733 890066
Website: www.youngwriters.co.uk

Book Design by Ashley Janson

SB ISBN 978-1-78203-498-8

Printed and bound in the UK by BookPrintingUK
Website: www.bookprintinguk.com

FOREWORD

Young Writers was established in 1991, dedicated to encouraging reading and creative writing by young people. Our nationwide writing initiatives are designed to inspire ideas and the incentive to write, and in turn develop literacy skills and confidence, whilst participating in a fun, imaginative activity. The final reward is the opportunity for the budding young writer to see their work in print.

Our latest competition, The Power of Poetry, focuses on learning about the different techniques and styles used in poetry and encouraging pupils to explore new ways to write a poem. Using poetry as their tool, the young writers were given the opportunity to express their thoughts and feelings through verse.

Whilst conveying their opinions through poetry, the writers showcased in this collection have simultaneously managed to give poetry a breath of fresh air, brought it to life and made it relevant to them. Using a variety of themes and styles, our featured poets leave a lasting impression of their inner thoughts and feelings, making this anthology a rare insight into the next generation.

Contents

Crown Primary School, Inverness

Inverallochy Primary School, Inverallochy

Kilcreggan Primary School, Kilcreggan

Knightswood Primary School, Knightswood

THE POEMS

Autumn Poem

Look at the lovely orange, green and red
All the nice colours on the trees and on the floor.
They are stunning
The bench looks lovely with the autumn leaves
I can hear all the birds chirping in the trees
I just can't imagine that it would be this lovely.
I feel like I'm in heaven
But I'm not.

Ryan Thomas Paterson (10)

My World

The moon is as white as the water that surges
and ripples below.

The sun is a lost shepherd with his lamp in the early
morning light looking for his flock.

The stars are chips of sea glass surfing on the black
swell of the morning tide.

The Earth is a blue and green paintball twisting and
wavering through an endless alleyway covered in dark
shadows.

Angus Stobo (11)

All Wrong

My mum wants me to be a gymnast
So I warned her I would end up in a cast
Double flip in a click, no way can I do that

My dad wants me to be a diver
So I try to be a skiver
I can't swim let alone dive in

My gran wants me to tap dance
Instead of play with the cat
1, 2, 3, 4; 1, 2, 3, 4, please, no more

My grandad wants me to play ping-pong
'How do you play?'
Is all I say and that is the end of that

Gymnastics, diving, tap and ping-pong
It is all wrong
I'd just rather read a book and cook.

Keala Jost (10)
Aberdeen Waldorf School, Aberdeen

Frosty Morning

F reezing, it's so cold
R obins are freezing in the trees
O ld trees are bare
S lippy, slippy on the frost
T oo snowy
Y ell, yell when I slip

M oon makes the trees sparkle
O ld trees are frosty
R ight, left, snow everywhere
N ew frost everywhere
I t's like the Ice Age
N ice new snow
G lowing trees.

Lucie Dow (6)
Armadale Primary School, Armadale

Frosty Morning

F rosty, frosty, I love frosty
R eally cold, are you cold?
O ld trees are bald
S lippy and slidey
T ry not to slide
Y es, I'm really cold

M ove your feet and step on the snow
O ther people where we should walk to
R obins jump on trees
N ight-time is coming, let's go to bed
I n the morning we are awake and making snowmen
N ight-time comes again and the moon comes out
G etting cold and you go inside.

CaCee McKenna (6)
Armadale Primary School, Armadale

Frosty Morning

F rosty mornings are cold
R obins jump on frosty branches
O bviously winter
S now is beautiful and shiny
T rees are sparkly in winter
Y ou yell when you slip

M ornings are bad enough without snow
O h! Always cold in winter
R eally cold
N ew snow is divine
I feel cold in winter
N ice, crispy snow
G littering snow.

Fraser Findlay (6)
Armadale Primary School, Armadale

Frosty Morning

F rosty on my fingers
R eally nipping at my nose
O bviously winter
S lipping and sliding to school
T rees are sparkly
Y elling when you slip

M ornings are snowy
O bviously winter
R eally nipping my nose
N ice when it is snowing
I gloo is my home
N ice when it is
G osh, it's cold.

Josh Skelton (6)
Armadale Primary School, Armadale

Frosty Morning

F rosty ground
R eally cold
O n the ice I slide and fall
S hivery morning
T oo cold
Y elling

M oon shining
O n the ice I am slipping
R obins bounce
N ice trees
I gloo is my new home
N ice, glittery snow
G littery trees.

Jack Edwards (6)
Armadale Primary School, Armadale

Frosty Morning

F rosty and snowy
R obins are hopping in trees
O ld trees are snowy
S now is slippy
T oes are frosty
Y elling is bad

M orning is snowy
O ld and rusty
R obins are freezing
N ose is frosty
I ce is freezing
N ew snow
G rass is away to snow.

Olivia White (6)
Armadale Primary School, Armadale

Frosty Morning

F rost on my fingers
R eally frosty here
O bviously it's freezing
S liding to school
T rees are sparkly with frost
Y ell when you slip

M ornings are frosty
O bviously it's freezing
R obins are red
N ice frost
I ce is slippy
N ice frost
G osh, it's cold!

Arran Waddell (5)
Armadale Primary School, Armadalo

Frosty Morning

F reezing today
R oad is slippy
O h, it is here
S now is coming
T oo cold
Y es, snow is here

M y mum is freezing
O h no, I can't find my gloves
R eally wish I could stay in bed
N ot hot
I cicles hanging from my window
N eed to build a snowman
G ood fun.

Stuart Cooke (5)
Armadale Primary School, Armadale

Frosty Morning

F rost on the ground
R eally cold
O h, the icicles
S lippery outside
T oday it is snowing!
Y ay, it is snowing!

M y hands are cold
O h no! Where are my gloves?
R eally! It is snowing!
N o, it's not hot, it's freezing cold
I t is icy in the morning
N ana is shivering
G igantic icicles.

Thomas Grieve (6)
Armadale Primary School, Armadale

Frosty Morning

F un going ice skating
R ather slippy
O h no! I forgot my gloves and my hat
S o cold
T ime to go inside
Y es, it is snowing

M y fingertips are cold
O ops, I slipped!
R eally cold
N o time to waste
I t's a good time to play
N ot good to play
G len was shivering in his room.

Cory Roberts (6)
Armadale Primary School, Armadale

Frosty Morning

F reezing snow on the ground
R eally, really cold
O h, I think I should go in
S illy me, I forgot to put on my gloves
T he snow is freezing today
Y ay, it's snowing!

M y hands are freezing and I'm shivering
O ops! I dropped my gloves again
R eally big icicles
N ah, don't go out there, it is cold
I n the garden it is freezing
N o snow yet
G ood, the snow is amazing.

Chloe Nicol (7)
Armadale Primary School, Armadale

Frosty Morning

F rost is so cold
R eally slippery today
O h, the icicles are sparkling
S nowing already
T oday it is so cold
Y ippee, I can make a snowman

M y hands are so freezing
O h no, my mum slipped on the ice
R eally icy, watch you don't fall
N ow it's time to play
I t's an icy morning
N ana's shivering
G igantic icicles.

Faith Paterson (7)
Armadale Primary School, Armadale

Frosty Morning

F reezing out here!
R obins on the ice stop cars
O h no! It is freezing
S top! Where are your hat and gloves?
T oo much ice!
Y ay! Let's have hot chocolate

M y mum put the fire on
O h no! the ice has broken
R ain, go away!
N ot going out in the snow
I t's deep that snow
N o sun today
G ood! Time for spring.

Eva McGrath (6)
Armadale Primary School, Armadale

Frosty Morning

F rosty morning already
R eally, really cold
O h, the icicles are sparkly
S now is here
T oday is my favourite day of the year
Y ay, my friends are playing in the snow

M y hat is still in the house
O h, my friend is hiding behind a frosty tree
R ain! No, I like snow
N o I don't want sun, I like snow
I f it snowed again I would be very happy
N othing is going to stop snow. I really like snow
G ran slipped on the ice.

Kerris Walton (7)
Armadale Primary School, Armadale

Frosty Morning

F un on the ice
R eally cold
O h no! I lost my gloves
S anta is coming
T ime for snow
Y esterday it was warm

M y car slipped on the ice
O h no, the snow has begun
R eally slippy
N o snow
I slipped
N o cars on the road
G ood time for snow.

Miroslaw (7)
Armadale Primary School, Armadale

Frosty Morning

F reezing cold
R eally icy
O h, the icicles are sparkling
S now is cold
T oday it is so cold
Y ay, I can make a snowman

M y hands are cold
O h, it is so cold!
R eally, it is snowing!
N o, it's not hot, it's freezing cold
I t is icy in the morning
N ana is shivering
G igantic icicles.

Toni Faulkner (7)
Armadale Primary School, Armadale

Frosty Morning

F reezing cold
R eally slippy outside
O h no, my dad says
S low down, it is icy
T oo late, it is snowing
Y ay, I love snow

M y teeth are chattering
O h no, the snow is melting
R emember when it was sunny
N o snow
I am having fun
N ot time for T-shirts
G ood. The ice has melted.

Jack Watson (7)
Armadale Primary School, Armadale

Frosty Morning

F reaking out
R eally cold and slippery
O h, there are snowballs!
S now, watch out, argh!
T here are lots of gigantic snowballs
Y ay, the snow is coming, great!

M y nose is solid, it's so cold
O h, I found my gloves
R oo's just slipped
N an, are your hands warm?
I cy all about
N o, I'm cold, Mum
G reat, the snow has stopped.

Jamie (7)
Armadale Primary School, Armadale

Frosty Morning

F rost! Great, this is exciting
R eally cold. It might snow
O h, here comes my teacher
S o sparkly and icy too
T oo cold, mmm what is that smell?
Y ay, it is snowing

M ornings are always cold
O h, it is so cold, I need something warm to eat
R eally good, I am going to make a snowball
N elly is shivering
I feel cold again
N o, I want it to be sunny now
G ood, the snow is still here, I don't really wish it was sunny.

Natalie McGhie (7)
Armadale Primary School, Armadale

Frosty Morning

F reezing cold family
R obin redbreast on the tree
O ctober it started to snow
S now
T he fish are frozen
Y ay, I love it

M um is freezing
O h no, I fell
R eally cold
N ana is shivering
I am freezing
N ever hot
G ood time to go inside.

Jamie Innes (7)
Armadale Primary School, Armadale

Frosty Morning

F rosty, cold morning
R eally cold, not hot
O h, someone was throwing a snowball at me
S now again
T oday it's snowing, oh yeah
Y es, I can make a snowman

M y tips of my fingers are cold
O h, what beautiful icicles
R ain, oh no
N ana is freezing cold
I 'm too cold
N ana, don't go out
G randad is cold.

Rebecca Paterson (6)
Armadale Primary School, Armadale

Frosty Morning

F rost all around me
R eally freezing here
O ld trees sparkle
S lipping and sliding on the way to school
T rees sparkling
Y elling in the snow.

Kayla Prentice
Armadale Primary School, Armadale

Frosty Morning

F reezing in the morning
R obins jumping
O ld trees sparkle
S liding on my bum
T rees are sparkling
Y elling.

Dale Berry
Armadale Primary School, Armadale

Frosty Morning

F rost is my favourite weather
R obins on branches
O ld frost is cold
S lidey paths on my feet
T oo cold, too cold to go outside
Y elling as I slip.

Robyn Ryce (6)
Armadale Primary School, Armadale

Frosty Morning

F ootprints in the snow
R obins hopping on the branches
O ld trees are bare
S lippy on the streets
T he trees are full of robins
Y elling when I fall on my bum.

Sarah Marshall (6)
Armadale Primary School, Armadale

Frosty Morning

F rosty morning
R eally cold morning
O ld trees are bare
S liding on the ice
T he ice is fun
Y elling because I fell on the ice.

Naomi Rollo (6)
Armadale Primary School, Armadale

Frosty Morning

F reezing fingers
R obins are jumping on the trees
O ld trees are bare
S nowflakes fall
T oes are freezing
Y elling when I fall on my bum.

Rhiannon Joyce (6)
Armadale Primary School, Armadale

Frosty Morning

F eels cold and frosty
R obins are red
O bviously cold
S lippy and slidey
T rees sparkle when the sun is out
Y ell when I slip and slide.

Chelsea Millen (7)
Armadale Primary School, Armadale

Frosty Morning

F rozen fingers
R obins are jumping
O ld trees are bare
S now is so sparkly
T he snow is falling
Y elling when I fall.

Millie Somerville (6)
Armadale Primary School, Armadale

Frosty Morning

F rozen fingers
R eally nippy on my nose
O bviously winter
S lippy and slidey
T here are snowflakes
Y es, it is frosty.

Elle Martin (6)
Armadale Primary School, Armadale

Frosty Morning

F ootprints in the frost
R obin bouncing on the tree
O bviously it is frosty
S lip on the ice
T rees are sparkly
Y elling when I slip on the ice.

Keiran Fisher (7)
Armadale Primary School, Armadale

Frosty Morning

F ootprints in the frost
R obins bounce on the branches
O ld trees are bare
S lippy on the frost
T rees are bare
Y elling when I fall.

Amy Tait (6)
Armadale Primary School, Armadale

Frosty Morning

F eels like it's the Ice Age here
R eally nipping my nose
O bviously winter
S now is falling
T rees are sparkly and bare
Y elling when I slip.

Caleb Mellors (6)
Armadale Primary School, Armadale

Olympics

I think the whole point of the Olympics is to win a gold
But trust me, they're all old.
The fastest man alive is Usain Bolt
And trust me, he could make a big moat.
The things that I like are with the bikes
And they're faster than trikes.
The opening ceremony is so much fun
The Olympic rings are as bright as the sun.
Mandarle and Wenlock are the two mascots
And they're both as strong as crocs.

Matthew Taylor (10)
Armadale Primary School, Armadale

Chocolate Cake

They are so yummy
In my tummy
When I was getting it out to bake
It all just has to break
I just love the flake on the top
I bought it from the shop
I just can't bear to make a mistake
After giving it a great big shake
When I got a birthday cake with a candle
My mum broke the door handle.

Teagan Cook (10)
Armadale Primary School, Armadale

Cakes

I made some cakes last night
It took a while but it was worth the fight.

I mixed the sugar and butter all around
At the end I was tired out.

I put the mix inside the cases
And put them in and turned it up to one hundred and eighty.

I took the cakes out the oven
And let them cool down till seven.

I put the icing on the cake
And I will eat one at quarter past eight.

I just ate a cake
And it tasted great!

Lesley-Anne Little (10)
Armadale Primary School, Armadale

Dogs

My dog has a bone
For when she is alone.

My dog is always muddy
And she comes in when I study.

My dog likes to jump logs
Even just to catch a frog.

My dog jumps
Over the speed bumps.

My dog would risk it
Just for a wee biscuit.

My dog likes to run
Just for a bit of fun.

Lisa Lloyd (10)
Armadale Primary School, Armadale

Reply To The Laddies!

Boys, you think you rule the school
But you're not that cool.

You flick your hair
But we don't really care.

You watch the telly too much
But you never clean the rabbit's hutch.

You've got a big fat belly
And a nose like a welly.

You're awfy annoying
And I think it's appalling.

Lucy Walker (10)
Armadale Primary School, Armadale

Spring, Summer, Autumn And Winter

In spring comes a lamb,
In winter they become beautiful ham.

In summer we play in the pool,
All because it's nice and cool.

In autumn, Halloween,
There's always a new Mr Bean.

In winter there is snow,
Oh, there is also a show.

And that happens every year,
Even if it is not here.

Emma Janet Glass (9)
Armadale Primary School, Armadale

Seasons

In the winter there is snow and it blows.
There is a glow in the sun
And now the sun is done.
In autumn the leaves fall,
So why don't you go to the mall?
Let's see the flowers grow,
So why are you saying no?
In summer there are flowers,
So you need to water them.
In the spring lambs and bunnies are born.

Zoe Tait (10)
Armadale Primary School, Armadale

My Cat Profile

Hi, I'm a cat called Gail
And I've got a big, fluffy tail
Also I've got big paws
And big, jaggy claws.

I like the way I purr
My mum says I've got nice fur
She also says I love a good munch
So that's why I always munch and crunch.

So I guess that's bye for now
So anyway . . . ciao!

Aimee Ferguson (10)
Armadale Primary School, Armadale

Fish, Oh Fish

Fish, oh fish,
You taste so good on a dish.
You are scaly,
And your name is Bailey.

You are hunted by a shark,
I could whack it on tree bark.
You always make your mark,
But you always get eaten by a shark.

You are floppy,
People think you are sloppy.
You are so good,
You make me in a good mood.

Emily Kilpatrick (11)
Armadale Primary School, Armadale

Football

On Monday at the hall
I was playing football

When I was playing I got a hook
Right up my foot

My mum says I am a wicked witch
When I play on the pitch

Listen to the crowd
They're so loud

Look at the holes
Because we've been scoring goals.

Taylor Cuthbert (10)
Armadale Primary School, Armadale

Frosty Morning

F lakes are sparkly
R obins are beautiful
O bviously winter
S nowflakes fall
T rees are bare
Y elling when you're hurt.

Kelsi Brown
Armadale Primary School, Armadale

We Will Remember

R emember the army
E very soldier dies
M en go to war
E veryone cried
M en were sent to battle
B lood flows
E ach man suffers in war
R emember the soldiers.

Charlie Casagranda (7)
Auchengray Primary School, Carnwath

We Will Remember

R emember the very big wars
E ach person had hope
M any men died in the war
E ven people who were not in the war remember
M emories of the men who died in the war
B attlefields spread with poppies
E veryone cried
R ed poppies to remember the blood that was spread.

Niamh Hastie (7)
Auchengray Primary School, Carnwath

We Will Remember

R emember my dad
E veryone cries
M en were sent to battle
E very child remembers the war
M en even remember World War I
B attlefields now have poppies on them
E ach suffers the death of war
R ed blood is the red poppies, black is to mourn.

Tom Wilson (8)
Auchengray Primary School, Carnwath

We Will Remember

R emember the 11th November
E very family is sad
M ay we remember the war
E ven children died
M en go to war
B attlefields have blood on them
E ach man suffers in war
R ed poppies came back to life after the war.

Kieran Keizars (8)
Auchengray Primary School, Carnwath

We Will Remember

R emember the poppies from the war
E very family cries and cries
M en die every day
E ach person cries
M any mothers cry
B attlefields full of poppies
E veryone cries
R ed poppies bloom.

Holly Baxter (7)
Auchengray Primary School, Carnwath

A Pencil's Work Is Never Done

At school all day and used all night,
A pencil is one to lead a life.

Black and yellow,
The colours of the school,
A pencil is striped in the new cool,
A hand hovers over it,
Ready to pounce,
The pencil is ready for its daily rounds.

Clenched by the stomach and now suffocating,
The pencil's ready for the making,
As it's shoved into the metal,
It screams in pain,
Like it's been stung by a nettle.

Left on the table,
Alone, abandoned and worked to the bone,
The rubbers shout, the rulers pout,
And the pencil smiles with joy.

Bethany Thomson (11)
Cleland Primary School, Cleland

The Monster Muncher

As he sat there on the table,
Dusty and tired
Waiting for his owner to awaken him.

The switch was flicked
And electricity ran through his veins.

His arms rolled up and switched off.
As the disc entered his mouth,
He hummed away,
Dreaming of what game he would play,
His name engraved on his shiny black coat.

Benjamin Lewis (11)
Cleland Primary School, Cleland

Brainy Bernard

Brainy Bernard, sitting on the desk,
Looking at the children,
Waiting to be fed.

His brain is always on,
Learning new things every day,
He's always hot from working,
He doesn't get to play.

His eyes, gleaming with glory,
He's desperate to tell them a story.
His excited heart, skips a beat,
When he hears the noise of approaching feet.

He fills his brain with new information,
People think what he can do is amazing.
But when everyone goes and the lights are turned off,
Lonely and silent, his eyes start to dull and his brain
Switches off.

Alisha Aslam (11)
Cleland Primary School, Cleland

Tick-Tock Tam

Tick-tock Tam,
Hanging on the wall,
Smiling with delight,
Waiting for a new day to start.

He ticks and he tocks,
And he never stops.

His heart starts to glimmer,
When people glance to tell the time.

He does not sleep, he does not cry,
I guess he's just a little shy.

As the sun disappears,
Tick-tock Tam is still ticking away,
Awaiting a new day.

Rachael Moffat (11)
Cleland Primary School, Cleland

The Hungry Washing Machine

The washing machine stares
As the kitchen's being cleaned.
He's waiting on his dinner
That is scrunched up in a basket.

He gets fed twice a day,
His cousin, the dishwasher 3.

He takes his food in all at once,
Spitting and throwing it about.

Once he has been fed, he spits his food out,
Every so often he gets a drink too.

His favourite meal by far is jeans and a jumper,
With a side of socks.

He goes to sleep tired,
Ready for the next day.
He is also very hungry,
Awaiting his next prey.

Darren Findlay (11)
Cleland Primary School, Cleland

Dance, Dance, Dance!

I love to dance,
When I get the chance.

I twirl and twirl,
And swirl and swirl.

I have class twice a week
And our moves are unique.

I dance jazz and ballet,
And I practise every day.

I dance around the house
And my ballet steps are as quiet as a mouse.

Our dancing show is yearly,
It's my favourite part, clearly.

To jazzy tunes we listen
And our costumes they do glisten.

The audience do cheer,
It's my favourite time of year.

Abbie Allen (11)
Colgrain Primary School, Helensburgh

My New Dog

I'm getting a puppy
In roughly 12 weeks.
I'm really excited,
How many more sleeps?

He will be black,
Maybe with white,
I can't wait to meet him,
It'll be love at first sight.

He's a Portuguese water dog,
He'll be perfect for me,
His coat doesn't shed,
He'll keep me allergy free.

He'll swim like a fish,
And have webbed paws too,
He'll go *splish, splash* and *splosh*
As he dives for a chew.

He'll greet me each day,
With a smile and a plea,
He'll say, 'I am glad to see you,
Please take me for a wee.'

I'm really looking forward
To having him at home,
I think it's time I finished now,
Thanks for listening to my poem!

Amy Andrade (11)
Colgrain Primary School, Helensburgh

Music Chorus

The instruments came together,
To make up a song,
The melody was finally ready,
As the drumstick counted them in.

The triangle was as pristine
As a clean house,
The glockenspiel was as
Soft as snow landing on a tree.

The clarinet and the flute
Came together like they were dancing gracefully,
The violin and the harp flew
Like two birds feeling euphoric.

The recorder started the chorus high,
As the trebles started off low,
Every instrument came together,
To make a tutti.

The drum was a loud
As a firework going off,
The cymbal crashed loudly,
Every third beat of a bar.

Their song was finally over,
Their hard work paid off,
They got a standing ovation,
When the last chord was struck!

Chiara Beaton (11)
Colgrain Primary School, Helensburgh

Le Frogs' Legs

'Bonjour monsieur, would you care to look at le menu?'
'Ah, bonjour garçon, oui merci.
Could I have le escargots?'
'Oui, we have got our snails freshly from Wales.'

'In fact, no!
Could I have le frogs' legs, s'il vous plait?'
'Ah, le frogs' legs!
Would you like this with some rotten eggs?'

'Non, non, that is a horrible!
Could I please have something a bit more tasty like the crème brulee lait?'
'And if we were in Spain,
We could say, ole!'

'That is it! That is it! I want to see Michel Roux, he will know what to do.'
'I'm sorry monsieur, he is not here, but I hear Raymond Blanc is near.'
'I do not want Raymond Blanc!
Och! Just get me a croissant.'

'And for refreshment I shall have le skinny latte.'
'Tut, tut, monsieur,
This is a fine dining restaurant,
Not a cheap take-away café!'

'Oh garçon, that is it, I have had enough!
I will bang this door shut,
And you can watch me walk away,
To *Pizza Hut!*'

Cameron Edwards (11)
Colgrain Primary School, Helensburgh

Gone

When sitting in the Anderson shelter
We hear the screaming bombs attack our family home
Laying its poisonous gases upon our burning house
As we step out into the bitter cold
We see no house there
. . . Gone

When standing in our decimated town
I see no buildings
No people, just rubble,
. . . Gone

When looking for people crushed under the rubble
I hear the screaming sirens of
Police vans and ambulances
Coming to the helpless people's rescue
The brave services hear an horrendous yell
'Help, my family are . . . gone!'

When saying goodbye to my family
And stepping on the train
I wonder to myself
How long will I be
. . . Gone?

When sitting on the chugging train
With my fellow evacuees
I think to myself, humanity
. . . *all gone!*

Heather MacDougall (11)
Colgrain Primary School, Helensburgh

Crutches

C runch goes the ankle
R olling over onto the ground
U p jumps my mum
T error written on her face
C alling for the ambulance
H elp appears soon after
E veryone watches as I'm loaded into the ambulance
S ix weeks on crutches, goodbye sport.

Murray Bissett (11)
Colgrain Primary School, Helensburgh

Dog Park

Puppies and dogs run around the park,
As they meet they begin to bark.
Owners talk to each other,
As the trees give them cover.
While the wind begins to sing,
The dogs' leads and collars go *ting, ting!*

The grass whistles a lovely tune,
While the caterpillars build a cocoon.
When his owner throws the ball,
The dog pretends it's tall.

The dogs jump in cheer,
When they finally reach here.
But when it's time to go,
The dogs howl, 'Oh no!'
But now it is getting dark,
It's time to leave the doggie park.

Emma-Lea Boyde (10)
Colgrain Primary School, Helensburgh

Goal!

The keeper's gloves catapulted the ball to the defender's feet
The Adidas stripes on his foot gently stroked the ball to the midfielder
The midfielder's foot cradled round the ball like a mother with her newborn baby
And then arrowed a pass to the opposite side of the pitch

A sudden burst of pace rocketed him up the line and then played an amazing through ball to the winger
His first touch was a sharp turn inside and then, *whoosh!*
He was so fast he nearly set the grass on fire
After some silky skill he crossed in an astonishing ball to the striker
At that moment everyone knew that only one thing would happen
Boom!
A brilliant volley on the edge of the box. Top corner.
Goal!

Jamie Grant (11)
Colgrain Primary School, Helensburgh

Wolf

Wolf makes me happy every day
When I visit him he loves to play
He's quite a big dog
With reddish-brown hair
And lovely green eyes that look everywhere
He likes to run and can run real fast
I try to keep up but I never last
He collects my granda and granny's post
A very smart dog, smarter than most
When I chap the door Wolf always howls
And if he doesn't know you he will growl
When he's ready for his walkies he goes to the door
With his leash in his mouth and dragging to the floor
Wolf is one of the best
That's why I love him more than the rest.

Nicole Haughie (11)
Colgrain Primary School, Helensburgh

My Dog Friend, Dougal

My pet dog is called Dougal,
He is my friend and makes me giggle,
He is funny and he is playful,
He's always there to give me cuddles.

His fluffy coat is white and brown,
Dougal's always there when I'm down,
His favourite food is chicken,
And he gobbles it up in seconds!

He dances when he gets his treat,
With his tail wagging when he eats,
Dougal loves to play in puddles,
And always gets himself in a muddle.

He loves to jump and loves to run,
But best of all he loves to dance.
His big, black eyes can almost talk,
And he loves to go for walks.

Dougal gets me through the hardest things,
Through summer, autumn, winter or spring!

Callum Hew (11)
Colgrain Primary School, Helensburgh

Snow Day

When I see the snow fall to the ground
It makes me feel warm all around.
As weird as that may seem,
But hey, that's just me.

I wrap up warm to go outside and play,
It is as though the snow is calling my name.

As the day comes to an end,
I am wet and soaking in,
My boots are full with snow up to my knees,
But if asked to come out again,
I would reply yes please.

Now I am told to go to bed,
But I sneak one last peek,
Watching the snow slowly thin.
But now it has gone
And left me feeling cold within.

With winter gone, I am sad within,
But I can truly say it was a winter
I really enjoyed playing in
And the day is over.

Maira Hussain (11)
Colgrain Primary School, Helensburgh

Match Away Day

I awake in the morning and I get up
I am ready to go and see my team play in the cup
Make my way downstairs for brekkie
Mum's making bacon and bread that's eggy

I get ready for the game
Pulling on my scarf and strip
Mum and I are ready for the away trip
We travel along the motorway in the car
Now I'm excited as it's not too far

We arrive at the ground and find our seat
The smell of the Bovril not so sweet
We are in the stand up at least 100 feet
I munch my pie and I'll get a bit stout
The teams make their way out
The crowd begins to bellow, I start to shout

The game kicks off
And the footballers start to play
Oh, what a game of excitement and dismay
My team scores and goes one up
There's every chance we can win this cup
Here's hoping I might get a wee sup

The game finishes, we win one-nil
The other team is out
And we're through to the final
Who will we play? No one can say
I'm looking forward to a winning away day!

Robbie Methven (11)
Colgrain Primary School, Helensburgh

Winter Days

I wake up shivering cold
Houses covered all with snow
Flinging snowballs at everyone
Making angels on the ground
Whilst snowmen dance up and down

I feel my fingers getting numb
I start to head home
As I walk through the door
I feel the warmth
My hands start to thaw

My mum brings me hot chocolate
As I sit at the fire
Keeping warm and cosy
Watching the snow fall.

Liam Robson (11)
Colgrain Primary School, Helensburgh

War

When most of the men are beginning
Some have already begun,
Their journey is almost ending,
Some are among their own end.

Even though they all have spirit,
The Nazis are just round the bend.
Men have lost lives, some of catastrophic
Injury that may be unable to mend.

By day they're out in the open,
By night they're like ghosts out to fright.

Then a hiss in the trenches,
People hide under the bed and the benches.

But now it's over, Hitler's been thrown over,
There's men back for their families' first kiss.

Charlie Macleod-Adams (11)
Colgrain Primary School, Helensburgh

Keep Calm And Carry On

Bombs fell whistling from the sky,
Families sat in Anderson shelters
In fear of what might happen
If Hitler was to win the war.
There would be people in camps
Armed with guards with dark hearts,
No mercy, no love.
Families woke up from a terrible dream,
As they heard no siren.
They went to go to their house,
But realised there was no house there.
Thinking to themselves,
Keep calm and carry on.

Trains whistled goodbye at the station
As children and parents made a pool of tears.
Children got on the train thinking,
What now? Will I ever see my parents again?
Is this the end for Britain? Is there no hope?
Then a boy stood up and said,
'Saying there's no hope is admitting defeat.'
The train lit up and everyone had hope,
They would fight back and *win!*

Children spread the word throughout the towns
To play their part and keep their faith.
The country would now prevail
And Germany's war machine would crumble.
After spreading the word,
Britain had all the courage they needed
And had the upper hand in the war
All
Because they kept calm and carried on!

Jack Ward (11)
Colgrain Primary School, Helensburgh

Music

Music is wonderful
And really very fun
When I play my clarinet
I feel like I could run

I like my CD player
It plays music all day
I try to get through all my songs
I really like Coldplay

I've almost finished my poem
And nearly all my songs
I think that I might stop now
Before it gets too long!

Kirsty Williamson (11)
Colgrain Primary School, Helensburgh

Equality

Equality looks like glass,
It is very delicate and can be easily broken.

Equality feels like the sun,
The comforting warmth of feeling like you belong.

Equality tastes sweet,
Like cake, shared equally between others.

Equality sounds like a calm beach,
The soothing sound of waves rushing into shore.

Equality smells fresh,
Like the smell of new beginnings.

If equality was an object, it would be a flower,
When a petal is missing it is not complete.

Equality is like a brick wall,
That we desperately need to keep up!

Freya Riddell (12)
Crown Primary School, Inverness

Equality - Cinquain

Respect
Friendship, kindness
Everyone is different
Love makes the world a better place
Respect!

Courtney Cathrine Davidson (11)
Crown Primary School, Inverness

Equality - Cinquain

Fruit bowl
Mixed together
We are all different
But we can live in harmony
And peace.

Seona MacBean (11)
Crown Primary School, Inverness

Equality - Cinquain

Respect
Equal loving
Fight for no racism
Together, achieve a lot more
Respect.

Mia MacDonald (11)
Crown Primary School, Inverness

Equality - Cinquain

Helping
Loving people
Sharing, balanced, caring
Finding harmony together
All equal.

Jack Baillie (11)
Crown Primary School, Inverness

Equality

People may be Muslim or Jewish,
They still deserve a chance,
People may be from Nepal or Texas,
They still deserve choice,
People may be 0 or 100,
They still deserve their say,
People may be black or white,
They still have feelings.

If equality was a food,
It would be evenly given out.
If equality was a sweet it would be jelly babies,
All different but delicious.
It would be a coin,
Both sides different but worth the same.

Jaime Robayna Gortazar (11)
Crown Primary School, Inverness

Football

Peaceful
Happy, joyful
Together, share, pass
Respectful, shake hands, smile
Be good, nice, no trouble, equality
Equal
No racism, be respectful.

Stefan Mackenzie Nicol (11)
Crown Primary School, Inverness

Equality - Cinquain

Countries
Different, balanced
Work together, happy
Determination makes a change
Countries.

Amy Fraser (12)
Crown Primary School, Inverness

Equality - Cinquain

Respect
A burst of warmth
All fight for human rights
Racism - unacceptable
Teamwork.

Will Maclean (12)
Crown Primary School, Inverness

Equality - Cinquain

Fairness
It's like a coin
Both sides are different
But with the same amount
Of worth
Caring.

Thomas Mcintosh (11)
Crown Primary School, Inverness

Equality - Cinquain

Fair trade
We are a team
Treating people fairly
Sharing out money equally
Respect!

Jade Paterson (11)
Crown Primary School, Inverness

Equality - Cinquain

Respect
Include others
Feelings are important
Everybody should get respect
Caring.

Aidan Ness (11)
Crown Primary School, Inverness

Equality - Cinquain

Fairness
Care for others
Respect everybody
Work together to achieve more
A team!

Sarah Calder (11)
Crown Primary School, Inverness

Equality - Cinquains

Why not
Countries on Earth
Put human rights in place
Doesn't matter about the skin
Valued

Passion
Understanding
Butterflies roaming round
Fresh, newborn flowers opening
Smiling

Success
Harmony, life
Working together, great
Everyone balanced on our Earth
Peaceful.

Catherine Low (12)
Crown Primary School, Inverness

Equality - Cinquain

Equal
Respect, belong
Together we achieve
Rights and responsibilities
Big team!

Jenny Blackwood (11)
Crown Primary School, Inverness

Rocket

R ockets going up to space. I wish I was there. I really do.
O h no! My toy rocket broke . . . where am I going to get another one?
C ounting up my money to see if I have enough.
K *aboom!* goes the rocket up into space, out into orbit it goes.
E nough money at last to buy a new rocket.
T en, 9, 8, 7, 6, 5, 4, 3, 2, 1 . . . and the rocket comes back safely at last!

Joel Joseph (9)
Crown Primary School, Inverness

Forest Trees

F rothing with plants, animals and most unique trees
O pen for free and never closes.
R earing up the deer dance
E verything is always happy as me!
S wishing trees that go with the whoosh of the wind
T rees high enough for a squirrel or for a bird

T rouble when they fall but calm in the wind
R esting every day but always moving
E very day and every night trees don't really give you a fright
E ventually they will die and everybody starts to cry
S adness will spread if they all fall down.

Munro Edwards (8)
Crown Primary School, Inverness

Hot Dogs

Porky, porky hot dogs
I love them so much
I eat them in my dreams
I see them in my thoughts
I have them for my lunch with
Onions and a little tomato sauce
I love them in my tummy
So yummy and scrummy.

Kevin Taylor (8)
Crown Primary School, Inverness

I Want A Rabbit

Rabbits look very fun
I very badly want one
But it might mess up the stairs
Or chew up all the chairs
I wouldn't be upset, if it wrecked my favourite dress
Or made a humungous mess
I would clean its cage every Friday
And after that we would play all day
I would feed it lettuce, carrots and treats
And watch the way it eats
Then tuck it up for bed
And stroke its little head

The reason I wouldn't be upset
If it wrecked my favourite dress
Or made a humungous mess
Is because my mother can stitch my dress
And clean up the mess
And sweep up the stairs
And buy new chairs
But I can't tell her this!
Do you promise not to tell her?
Because if you do I will never get a rabbit!

Jennifer Macknight (9)
Crown Primary School, Inverness

Sweet

S weets are delicious but some are disgusting!
W hen you go to the dentist you'd better watch out!
E very day you should brush your teeth at least two times a day.
E very day you must eat fruit!
T eeth can get pulled out and it will be painful! 'Argh!'

Jessica MacLellan-Hawkes (10)
Crown Primary School, Inverness

Pop Star

Have you met a pop star?
Do you know what they are like?
I really mean from the inside
What kind of feelings do you get?
Is it all just one big threat?
Do they live in mansions
Or little caravans?
Do they live with their band?
I have asked so many questions
I should have found out
Yesterday!

I guess we are all different
I mean to say
Pop stars are pop stars
And that's what they say.

Sasha Webb (9)
Crown Primary School, Inverness

The Sun Is Bright

The sun is bright
The sun is fun
You might not know how hot the sun is
But I bet it is very hot
I can't tell you how hot the sun is because I don't know
The clear blue sky, no clouds in sight
All I think about are summer days
My mum sunbathes and I play with my friends
I go into the kitchen and get some strawberries and they are so good
My cat, Rosie, comes out and lays under the sun
Yum!
These strawberries are so good!
I say goodbye to all my friends, then it's time to sleep.

Rebecca MacLennan (8)
Crown Primary School, Inverness

Kittens

K ittens, fluffy like white clouds in our blue, beautiful, bright sky
I n the SSPCA you can get one or two cats or small kittens
T all or big and small is the choice you can make
T hey trust you, believe you, love you, are their friend!
E at and sleep . . . they do play with you forever
N ever torture kittens or other animals. If you do they will have to take it and then you have to pay
S ince you are there for them, they will be there for you!

Karolina Waskowiak (9)
Crown Primary School, Inverness

Magic

Potions and lotions and hexes and spells
Witches and wizards and bad-smelling smells
Wands go with wizards and broomsticks with cats
Wicked old witches with shrivelling hats
Alice in Wonderland with the Hatter having tea
Ooh, who is that in the sky?
Wow, it's Nanny McPhee!

Back to the future with Marty and the Doc
Off with Harry and Hermione and Ron
What about Ginny and Luna - they're gone!
Levitating white feathers and rainbows of gold
Invisibility cloaks and quills to hold.

Abracadabra, alacazam, some say abraxas
Some say shazam
Whatever your potion, whatever your spell
However you say it, say it well!

Magic is the dawn in the morning
Beautiful to behold
At the end of the rainbow
Look for a pot of gold!

Elissa Hunter-Dorans (8)
Crown Primary School, Inverness

Healthy Food

H ealthy? Stay healthy with lovely vegetables
E very piece of fruit helps your bones to grow tough and strong
A pples grow on lovely trees in your beautiful garden
L ive longer if you eat delicious fruit
T o live a happier life, fruit is the thing for you
H appy with your life? Make it even better with luscious fruit
Y ou have to trust me, it's brilliant!

F or a more active life, fruit will do a brilliant job
O ranges have some sugar in them so don't eat too many even though it is very hard
O atmeal is a lovely thing to have for breakfast with some fruit at the side
D ads make delicious salads so remember to ask him for some occasionally.

Ryan MacLennan (9)
Crown Primary School, Inverness

Halloween Horrors

Halloween is here today
Halloween we fear to say,
Zombies creeping in your room
Soon you'll hear a big, loud *boom!*
Witches waving their big, white wand
Here comes the Bogeyman from the pond.

I see a group of skeletons
I see some moving Wellingtons,
Do I see a big, white ghost?
Oh no, he is delivering some post.
Stay away from vampires too
Wolves and werewolves might see you!

Orla Amos Davidson (10)
Crown Primary School, Inverness

The Bonfire

Fizz! Bang!
All the children sang,
'It's Bonfire Night!'

Crackle! Whizz!
You would not want to miss
Bonfire Night!

Wow! Pow!
'Buy some fireworks now
Because it is Bonfire Night!'
Green, red
All the people said,
'It's Bonfire Night!'

Keiran McBride (10)
Crown Primary School, Inverness

The Devil

Are you brave enough to meet him?
Are you brave enough to meet him?
Are you brave enough to meet the Devil?
Because on every Halloween night
If you hear a *bang*
Then that's the Devil's sigh.

He'll wiggle his tail like a happy puppy
But that means he's planning something bad.
Like socking you until you freeze
Or he'll zoom past you like the wind
And turn you into an ice statue.

If he laughs loud
Or you might hear
A trumpet or a drum
Then that was him
Doing a trick on you!
Beware of the Devil
'Cause he might be round the corner.

Karolina Kunicka (10)
Crown Primary School, Inverness

Littlemill Orienteering

I went orienteering,
At Littlemill,
I had to keep on peering,
Over the hills.

The controls were hard,
The course was long,
When you thought you were right,
You'd be wrong.

I went orienteering,
At Littlemill,
I had to keep on peering,
Over the hills.

I struggled and stumbled,
On number nine,
But even when you're wrong,
Don't you whine,
'Cause you'll be fine!

Ronan Blackwood (10)
Crown Primary School, Inverness

Garry The Ghost

Garry the ghost galloped past
So excited not to be last
Of all the ghosts on his street
And other people he would meet

On the way he saw his friend
When he skipped round the bend
All the way he thought a lot
About gruesome goodies to fill his pot!

Elena Hilferty (10)
Crown Primary School, Inverness

Sting

Sting glows blue when Orcs
Are near
Sting is clear with
Swirls on the blade.
The blade is as silver as a star.
And the handle is as brown
As an oak tree.
It was found in a cave, then it was saved.
It fought giant spiders in Mirkwood.
It fought really good
That's how it came across the name Sting.

Jamie Kinsey (10)
Crown Primary School, Inverness

Snow Is Everyone's Favourite Time Of Year

S now is everyone's favourite time of year
N ow the family is sitting by the warm cosy fire
O h, it sounds like the birds are singing, oh my dear turn your light out and sleep with the birds singing in your mind
W inter nights, freezing nights, makes snow fall again
I love snow so much
N ever forget my dream is snow, I love you snow and that will never change
G row, snow grow. You mean so much to me

Growing is my favourite thing to do but not as much as my family loves me
Ending my heart is never going to happen
Memories are going to happen in summer but it is never the end.

Molly Dickson (9)
Crown Primary School, Inverness

Anger

Anger, anger it makes you red
Especially when you're told to go to bed
It makes you want to clench your fists and then rub your wrists
My head is banging, my eyes are bulging, I want to scream and scream, ooh
I waken, thank goodness! It was only a dream.

I get up and stub my toe on the end of my bed
Oh I can feel the anger rising in my head.
I go and get my breakfast but there is not any left
That is why my brother had a smirk on his face
I am so angry I run up stairs and I slam the door behind me
I pull the duvet off my bed and just scream and scream and scream!

Carly Fraser (8)
Crown Primary School, Inverness

My Cat Can Play The Harp

My cat can play the harp
And that is really strange
I think she got the harp lessons when I started to play

She knows all the strings
A, B, C, D, E, F and G
There's no way she's coming
To harp lessons with me!

My cat can play the harp
And that is for a start
But when she takes a bowl of milk
She starts to fart!

Shanay Elmas (9)
Crown Primary School, Inverness

Dolphins

D own there, the dolphin hides in the sea
O h no! People run before they come and eat you now!
L oud rocks crack as the sharks eat the fish
P hones, handbags, float in the sea from the shark's sharp teeth. Don't look back, they're coming to eat you!
H ow will we save ourselves? Oh look! The dolphin comes and saves us. Cool!
I love dolphins, they're very helpful, sometimes never hunt for sharks
N ow that you have learned your lesson don't do it again!

Niki Simeonov (9)
Crown Primary School, Inverness

Drawing

I love to draw, oh yes I do.
My pencil glides across the paper.
Making marks on the page.
I wish to do my best on a fantastic drawing,
My drawing on the wall
Of my bedroom.

Ben McIntosh (8)
Crown Primary School, Inverness

Waves On A Beautiful Day

I hear the waves
Crashing like a brick tumbling down
Smashing down like thunder and lightning
Gurgling and glugging
A mini tsunami heading towards the shore.

I see the waves
Flying and flinging seaweed
Washing up pieces of driftwood and creels.
Hitting and splitting, weakening the rocks
Turning and twisting, darting and parting sharp rocks
Finally hitting the shore.

The waves remind me of
A plane preparing for landing.
The tsunami in Japan
That people have made.
A spaceship plunging into the sea like
Whizzing and hissing
Waving and roaring
Pouring and roaring
Running and stunning
Dripping and skipping
Dropping and hopping
Hitting and spitting
Meteor hitting the water.

Steven-James Bowie (11)
Inverallochy Primary School, Inverallochy

What Is The Moon?

The moon is like a chalk-white
asteroid dropped from deep space

It is like a dimmed light bulb
in the night sky that doesn't go out until day comes

The moon is like a blue firework waiting to explode
when day comes to become sun

It is like a silver bright knight in shining armour
guarding the night sky from monsters

The moon is like a shining grey owl
hunting for its prey as it looks through the midnight sky.

Charlie Coltherd (11)
Inverallochy Primary School, Inverallochy

What Is The Moon?

The moon is a silver banana
Shining in the magic night sky

It is a crystal ball
With its beautiful reflection on the sea

The moon is a bunch of glimmering angels
All grouping together to make a round, bright light

It is a roll of shiny wrapping paper
Covering a bouncy ball

The moon is an emotional face
That vanishes when daylight approaches us.

Lianne Wisely (10)
Inverallochy Primary School, Inverallochy

Wave's Stormy Day

I can hear moaning and groaning like an alien trying to speak
Sand scraping while the sea pushes away
Crashing and smacking of the sand hitting the sand
Waves screaming and shouting
Sea with crunching shells
Like a scraping of pebbles.

Waves pushing closer and closer to my feet
A breaker with bubbles heading towards me
More bubbles as the waves get higher
Water crashing against the rocks like a glass of water
Getting spilt over the rocks.

The waves remind me of thunder and lightning hitting trees
Like a hosepipe hitting dangerous rocks
A building collapsing from a tsunami.

The waves are . . .
Moaning and groaning
Rumbling and crumbling
Wrinkling and twinkling
Beaming and steaming
Tossing and crossing
Evolving and revolving
Blending and mending
Thundering and wondering
Slapping and patting
Crashing and mashing
Whizzing and hissing
Rumbling and tumbling
This is what the waves do on a stormy day.

Alice Brannan (10)
Inverallochy Primary School, Inverallochy

Waves On A Stormy Day

When I go to the shore
I hear the waves
Crashing onto the rocks
And whistling like the wind

When I am at the shore
I see the waves
As curved as a tap
I see white bubbles
On top of the waves
I see green and blue
Tin foil I see
The waves crashing
Full force

The waves remind me of
Water bubbling in a pot
And building up each day
Reminds me of a ghost
Then curves into water

What are the waves like
At Inverallochy and Cairnbulg?
Fighting and crashing
Clashing and bashing
Glittering and shimmering
Gleaming and shining
Battling and rattling
Foaming and steaming
Jumping and lumping
Glittering and filtering
Darkling and sparkling

This is the waves
At Cairnbulg and Inverallochy.

Chloe Murray (11)
Inverallochy Primary School, Inverallochy

What Is The Moon?

The moon is like a frozen, mischievous spaceship
Looking down at Earth,
Waiting peacefully to invade.
The moon is a mischievous spaceship.
The moon is like a ball of ice melting slowly away
Into the dark, cold night.
It is a melting ball of ice.
The moon is like a diamond put down
On a deserted sea of death.
It is a diamond on a sea.
The moon is like a silver, glimmering circle
Painted on a piece of dark card.
It is a glimmering circle.
The moon is like a magical full stop in the sky
Suffering thunder and savage winds.
It is a full stop in the sky.

Clarissa Johnston (10)
Inverallochy Primary School, Inverallochy

What Is The Moon?

The moon is a shimmering disco ball
Glowing in the night sky
It is a cold, bright, round ice cube
Melting away in daylight
The moon is a gigantic, glittering sphere
Diminishing in the clear blue sky
It is a bunch of twinkling stars
Grouping together to make a dazzling sight
The moon is a scoop of vanilla ice cream
Splattered on top of a murky, navy piece of paper.

Annie Mo Buchan (10)
Inverallochy Primary School, Inverallochy

The Waves

I hear striking waves battling against the deep blue sea
Gigantic waves crashing onto the slimy rocks
Freezing cold waves making their way in to shore quickly
Waves sound like an angry monster rising towards the hard sand.

I see waves making white, bubbly, fluffy foam
Heading towards the crunchy sand
Dark shaded blue rising higher and higher
A big, blue, hungry cloud demolishing all in sight.

A basin full of water being shaken side to side
A big lake on a nasty, horrible Tuesday
A white cloud on a rough day
The waves are like a roaring beast on a stormy, horrible, rainy Friday.

The waves are . . .
Roaring and demolishing
Freezing and battling
Striking and growing
Moving and rising
Shrinking and dying.

That's how the waves growl on a stormy day.

Jenna Ritchie (12)
Inverallochy Primary School, Inverallochy

What Is The Moon?

The moon is like a beam of illumination
Shooting peaceful reflections on the frothy ripples of the sea

It is like a vacuum
Diminishing all the delightful daylight

The moon is like a mirrored disco ball
Gliding elegantly in mid-air

It is like a million stars
Colliding together to make one big, white light bulb

The moon is like a silver dress
Abandoned in the dark night sky.

Kelly Stephen (12)
Inverallochy Primary School, Inverallochy

What Is The Moon?

The moon is like vanilla ice cream
On top of a freshly made waffle cone

It is like a snowball biscuit
That's rock-solid with black coconut sprinkled on top

The moon is like a belly on a snowman
Increasing immensely in size

It is like a circle of cheese
Made freshly from the butcher's getting ready to eat

The moon is like a white owl moving
Closer by the minute like an astronaut.

Kyuss Cardno (11)
Inverallochy Primary School, Inverallochy

Waves On A Stormy Day

I can hear lions roar as the waves come in
Then a ripple of comfort going out to sea
Thundering of rocks as the waves go back.
I can see waves all shapes and sizes
White horses of the sea
Little sparkles of glitter in the waves
Like a snowflake touching the tips of the waves of the ocean
Like a blue ruler gliding around Earth.
So dreamy that I felt as though
I was getting pulled out to sea
As cold as an ice cube as I enter the ocean
The waves remind me of
A painting of a fairy tale.
A white aeroplane flying low
Things can be calm one minute
And rough another minute.
The waves as they appear . . .
Hitting and splitting
Roaring and rolling
Bashing and crashing
Flowing and foaming
Drifting and lifting
Waving and raving
Smashing and sweeping
Creeping and leaping
Flowing and blowing
Darting and parting
Collecting and projecting
Sparkling and darkening
Frothing and rolling
Glowing and lightening
Freezing and breezing
Drizzling and pouring
Roaming and growing
Moaning and groaning
Glittering and frittering.

All of these things
I don't have to walk that far to see them.

Emma Masson (10)
Inverallochy Primary School, Inverallochy

Waves On A Stormy Day

I heard the crashing waves
Bashing against the shells and rocks.

I heard the smashing waves
Gathering into the land.

I see waves skimming
The top of the water.

The waves were battering
Against the solid, hard rocks.

I think waves remind me of
Me and my sister arguing over something stupid.

The waves are like
Fairy liquid because it looks like
The green colouring with foam and blue.

Waves are like a flushing toilet
Swirling round the sea.

Waves are like a puzzling puzzle
That you can't jump over.

Waves are like a roaring monster
Waiting to eat somebody up.

The waves are crashing and dashing,
Slapping and twisting,
Curling and whirling,
Flushing and hissing,
Roaring and puzzling,
Wrenching and horrifying,
Never-ending but
Always there doon at
The shore.

Caitlyn Masson (11)
Inverallochy Primary School, Inverallochy

Waves

I can hear
The churning of water,
The rushing of life-threatening waves,
The thunder of rock on a stormy day.

I can see
Caves forming in the water,
They are like a pride of mighty lions,
Towering high then dismantling,
A surge of white wasps.

The waves remind me of huge buildings towering skywards,
Of magnificent horses rearing on their burly hind legs
A cauldron bubbling and writhing

Waves growing,
Waves increasing,
Foaming and roaming,
Rushing and crushing,
Speeding and fleeing,
Tossing and turning,
Bashing and crashing,
Smashing and mashing,
Jumbling and tumbling,
Shaking and quaking,
Blocking and flocking,
Surging and raging,
Going on and on like the pace the world spins,
Blasting and lasting,
Flinging and flicking,
Frothing and raving,
Engorging and encrusting,
Trekking and cloning,
Racing and tracing,
Battling and beating,
Charging and raging,
Retreating and whipping,
Blocking and thickening,
Soaring and soaking,
Roaring and sailing,
Glittering and gleaming,
Cunning and running,

Swarming and storming,
Whisking and frisking,
Coming and going,
Swelling and dwelling,
Wrecking and drenching,
Curving and rampaging,
Collecting and ascending,
Imposing and circling,
Boating and splashing,
Defending and attacking,
Moaning and groaning,
Bumping and jumping,
Spinning and stunning,
Destroying and dismantling,
Detaching and hatching,
Jerking and working,
This is the way the waves all move,
Unique in every way.

Stuart Biegala (11)
Inverallochy Primary School, Inverallochy

What Is The Moon?

The moon is an outstanding white plate
Floating in the midnight sky

It is a jet-black bolt
That is resting for another night

The moon is a formidable creature
Stalking in the night

It is the unfortunate longing light
Of the shadowy world

The moon is a bomb dwelling in space
That will soon create a catastrophe.

Arron Masson (12)
Inverallochy Primary School, Inverallochy

Waves On A Stormy Day

I hear
Blue waves crashing on the rocks
Waves flowing to a rhythm with the wind
Slapping the yellow sand
Crunching, as it pulls the sand into the vast sea.

I see
Tall piers being sprayed with water
Rock pools overflowing
Waves creating huge explosions of sand
Like fireworks on the 5th of November
Pearl-white horses racing on the crest
Seagulls floating up and down
Squawking in terror like a horror film

It reminds me of
Climbing a big mountain
Battling to the snowy top
Watching a fountain
Spraying the people, examining its complex pattern
The waves are like a bonfire
Sparks flying everywhere
Spray whipped cream
Being squirted into a bowl of blue food colouring
Being eaten as the foam washes away
It is like the black night sky
With yellow and white starfish acting as stars

The waves on a stormy day are
Smashing, thrashing, lashing, bashing
Laying, spraying
Sobbing and bobbing
Then they start whirling, twirling
And then curling
Evolving, revolving, solving
Ascending then descending
Defying, supplying, crying
Slapping, clapping, antagonising, surprising
Glistening, listening
Then sneaking and creeping.
Protruding, subduing, retrieving, deceiving
Going, foaming

Slowing, roaring,
Spraying and saying
Then it starts flooding and bubbling
And banging and twanging
Speeding, leading, screaming
Then finally crunching and munching.

But then it starts ranting and grunting
And moaning and groaning
Then thundering and blundering
Losing and choosing
Falling and brawling
Sighing and lying.

It's calming down
With the peaceful breeze.

Georgia Morrison (11)
Inverallochy Primary School, Inverallochy

What Is The Moon?

The moon is like the Mercedes badge
On the front of a massive black car
It is like a luminous torch
Lighting up the empty sky
The moon is like a pearl-white, fluffy snowball
Being thrown up in the air
It is like a mushroom with a white top
The grass transformed into a dark blue sky
The moon is like a first-rate watch
Strapped round a wrist of space.

Lewis Noble (10)
Inverallochy Primary School, Inverallochy

Waves On A Stormy Day

I can hear the rushing of
The waves crashing against
The seashore as if it is the
Downpour of a waterfall.

When I am at the shore
All I can see is the very top
Of the waves.

The waves are so noisy
But so relaxing it is like a
PJ day but at the shore.

The waves are always there for me to see
But I must time it just right
Because sometimes
It is not windy enough.

Waves are so creepy
Because they always
Come running up to shore.

It is amazing to see the waves
Drifting across the magnificent sea.

The wind makes the waves roar
Like a sea lion.

The waves are a part of my mind of my life
Because I live really near the shore.

The waves remind me of a cold bubble bath
That is overfilling with bubbles.

Bubbling and flowing
Drifting and rushing
Whizzing and hissing
Turning and twisting
Shining and speeding
Dripping and speeding
Mooning and groaning
Bumping and jumping

Splashing and clashing
Curling and whirling
Gliding and sliding
Dashing and flashing.

This is the way that waves are to me.

Nicole Grant (10)
Inverallochy Primary School, Inverallochy

What Is The Moon?

The moon is like a cherished silver tray
Being despatched to the imperial king.

It is like a silver sheet of circular paper
Glued to a cloudy piece of dark blue card.

The moon is like a torch beaming down on us
To light up the gloominess of the universe.

It is like a drifting boat
Across the intense ocean to become the enchanted moon.

The moon is like a white goose drifting up the sky
And halts for a violent stop.

Isla Stephen (11)
Inverallochy Primary School, Inverallochy

Waves On A Stormy Day

I hear waves hissing through the town
Like a gigantic thunderstorm blowing everywhere
Wind blowing at the waves
And splashing at the rocks
No one is in the town.

All I see are waves rising up,
Getting higher and higher.
The waves jumping high
Like a gymnast on a trampoline.
Waves straggling against the force
Of the Loch Ness monster
As he rages from the water . . .
Going on a boat when
It is so windy outside, idiotic!

The water moves away quickly
But returns as fast as it left
In preparation to fight and splash
Everywhere.
Looking at the waves
That are coming towards me
I feel very frightened
And scary and dirty,
Slimy and shocking,
Splashing,
The day was almost as dark as night!

Leaping and creeping,
Rocking and hitting,
Speeding and spinning,
Skipping and splitting,
Twisting and frisking,
Whisking and hissing,

Dramatic waves crashing,
Dancing and jumping,
Clashing and slapping
And playing.

Joe Cardno (12)
Inverallochy Primary School, Inverallochy

My Wonderful Nephews

How small one is
He is so beautiful to look at
When he opens his eyes

One is tall and fast
He is very funny
And very sunny

My nephews are wonderful
One is one year old
And one is two weeks old
Whether laughing or crying
Walking or sleeping
They are the very best.

Alice Dryburgh (11)
Kilcreggan Primary School, Kilcreggan

Animals

Animals, animals everywhere
Jumping, flying, galloping without a care
Animals are fun so everyone says

Bunnies are cute
Bees are noisy
Hedgehogs are prickly
Butterflies are colourful
Horses are friendly

Guinea pigs are chatty
Hamsters are fluffy
Koalas climb trees
Snakes slither around
Pandas are cuddly

Animals, animals everywhere
Hope all our owners look
After them with lots of love
And care.

Murrin Macgregor (11)
Kilcreggan Primary School, Kilcreggan

A Game Of Netball

Netballers on their toes,
Then suddenly the whistle blows,
They all race to the centre of the hall,
To get their hands on the ball.

The blue team get the ball,
But in front the red team stand tall.
The blue team loses the ball,
The giant reds quickly pass.

The ball makes its way to the shooter,
She has two hands on the ball.
Silence throughout the hall,
All eyes on the ball.

Her toes leave the ground,
She can hear no sound,
Then in it goes,
Still standing on her toes.

The crowd are clapping,
Both hands slapping,
The crowd
Is very loud.

Hannah Anderson (10)
Kilcreggan Primary School, Kilcreggan

Thunder And Lightning

The forked devil that shakes the night
The thunder rumbles, the clouds crumble in fright
The inevitable flash that you've been dreading
The bloodcurdling strike that turns buildings to shreddings

While Zeus rages above the storm
The intricate music from thunder is born
But while the clouds are crying
And the storm is eventually dying
No one will forget the thunder and lightning!

Arran Dunbar (11)
Kilcreggan Primary School, Kilcreggan

Animals

Animals are sweet
Animals are kind
They're always on my mind

Cats, dogs and hedgehogs
I like them so much

Dogs are fun, active and energetic
To run with them you have to be athletic

Creeping cats chasing mice
They love to play with my fluffy dice

Hedgehogs are prickly with snuffly noses
Fluffy tummies sniffing at roses.

Erin McNeilage (10)
Kilcreggan Primary School, Kilcreggan

Boom Go The Fireworks

Boom go the fireworks
What a glorious sight.

Fireworks are bright
They light up the night
What a brilliant sight.

Wrap up, it's cold outside!
In my home snug and tight
Enjoying this fantastic night.

People cheering, people shouting,
Saying, 'More, more, more!'
But silence, no more fireworks!

Jamie McKnight (9)
Kilcreggan Primary School, Kilcreggan

Koalas

Koalas are cuddly
Koalas are cute
They climb the trees
Past honeybees

He will keep going, till he makes
It past all of the snakes
Fall out onto the shed
Land on his fluffy head

Eat the mushrooms on the shed
Then rub the bump on his head
Fall off and he will pass
A door before he hits the grass

Crawl off into the forest
Past a rabbit who is very modest
Climb the tree with a moan
Into his little home.

Lewis Smith (10)
Kilcreggan Primary School, Kilcreggan

I Can't Write A Poem

I can't write a poem
My brain is too busy thinking about . . .
Not writing poems.
There are holes in my jotter
I can't do it!
My writing skills have deserted me
My arms have stopped working
I can't see the words
Anyway, my brain isn't programmed . . .
For writing poems.
What do you mean I've written a poem?
No! No! I didn't want to write a poem
No way! I actually did it.

Daniel Main (10)
Knightswood Primary School, Knightswood

My Teacher

My teacher is amazing
I like it when she starts to teach
But the only thing I don't like is
Her long, long speech

Sometimes she is shouty
Like when she shouts out 'James'
The only thing that happens is
She bursts into flames

It really is annoying
When it comes to pain
She can't really do it
So she always has to faint

When it comes to maths
She is really glad
I think it is because
We are not that bad

My teacher is weird
When she acts like a fool
And I know that
She can be cool

I can't wait till home time
It's the last day of school
I can play video games
And also say I rule.

Daniel Lyasota (9)
Knightswood Primary School, Knightswood

Sadness

Sadness is a light blue
It smells like something died inside
It tastes like Brussels sprouts that have gone bad
It sounds like a river overflowing with tears
It feels like a drizzle of darkness
It lives in the deepest, darkest of forests.

Layla Willow Wilson (9)
Knightswood Primary School, Knightswood

Winter

Freezing cold air,
Whistling through my fingers,
Cold icicles,
Hanging from my nose.
Warm, swirly hot chocolate,
Drizzling down my throat,
Roast potatoes
Cooking in the kitchen.
Santa sending out presents,
Beautiful rainbow snow cones,
Sitting beside the fire,
That's what I call winter.

Holly Hanlon (10)
Knightswood Primary School, Knightswood

I Can't Write A Poem

I can't write a poem
I'm doing my work
My pencil ran away
A tiger ate my jotter
The war is nearly over
The world is about to end
A giraffe ate my pencil
A baby sat on my jotter
What do you mean I've written a poem?
OMG, I'm shocked!

Iona Sarah Izatt (9)
Knightswood Primary School, Knightswood

Summer

On my way running along the beach
Looking up at the golden sun
The blazing hot nights make me sweat
Crabs scuttling across the beach
Steaks sizzling on a barbecue
A perfect holiday in Spain
Sun blazing through the windows
School's out
The beautiful sunset setting over the sea.

Ewan Stark (9)
Knightswood Primary School, Knightswood

Zombies

Eating random body parts,
They make me want to puke.
They sometimes show up at night.
I stand stock still in fear.
They sometimes want to fight.
They come in through the windows
And gobble you up in one bite.

Graham Brown (9)
Knightswood Primary School, Knightswood

Roller Coasters

Roller coasters speeding past,
Roller coasters going past,
Loop-the-loops and twirls and spins,
Sudden stops and going backwards.
Painted red or orange or green,
Scarier than Halloween,
My stomach goes up while I go down,
I would rather be in town.
Butterflies are in my tummy,
And I am shouting, 'Help me, Mummy!'

Amy Docherty (9)
Knightswood Primary School, Knightswood

The Scream

I can hear horrifying screams
Even in my dreams.
There's a glowing red
Under my bed.

Argh! I see a mummy
Something wrong in my tummy.
I'm beginning to fall
Hearing nothing at all.

Then I hit the ground
Hear screams all around.
I really need a friend
Could this be the end?

James Laurie (9)
Knightswood Primary School, Knightswood

My Dad

I love my dad
He's a really great lad
He builds things all day
Has no time to play
He works until eight
And picks me up late
But when he's back
He's always on track
My dad's a cool dude
And treats me real good.

Sophie Anne Murray (10)
Knightswood Primary School, Knightswood

Love

Love is a pure pink
It smells like rose petals and lavender
It tastes like strawberry cupcakes
It sounds like sweet music
It feels like the beginning of new life
It looks like one million little kisses
It lives in a beautiful palace.

Paige Martin (10)
Knightswood Primary School, Knightswood

I Can't Write A Poem

I can't write a poem
My budgie stole my jotter
I fell in a hole in the floor
I got hit by a football
I lost my fingers
My jotter got burnt
Anyway, how do you write one?
What? I've written a poem?
Ugh, all those excuses for nothing!

Adam Robert Bulloch (9)
Knightswood Primary School, Knightswood

My Sister

My sister is fun
She loves to run
She's good at art
And really smart
And has an invisible friend
Called Bart
She's four years old
And really bold
I love my little sister.

Amy Egan (9)
Knightswood Primary School, Knightswood

I Can't Write A Poem!

I can't write a poem
I'm Mary Queen of Scots
My jotter is on fire
A ninja took my face
Mrs Martin can't afford pencils
My chair is on fire
There's a pig in the classroom
Anyway, I don't approve of poems
What do you mean I've written a poem?
Yippee! Yippee! I'm so happy!

Teigan Donaldson (9)
Knightswood Primary School, Knightswood

In My Bed

In my bed
He'll come and get me
Nobody knows where he lives
He roars with laughter every night
The venomous creature knows no fear
Born to torture children
A catastrophe in my mind
When he's around.

Mason Walter Matthew MacFarlane (10)
Knightswood Primary School, Knightswood

The Dark!

Opening my eyes at night
Suspicious dark figures on my wall
Screams coming from outside
Trees tapping on my window
Moans coming from the other side of my door
Hairs on the back of my neck stood on end
I freeze on the spot with fear
White as a snowman
Something crawling up my leg
I turn on the light and there is nothing there.

Benjamin Morrick Hamilton(9)
Knightswood Primary School, Knightswood

Morning

As the sun rises
We start to wake up
A new day dawns
We put on our make-up
We eat our breakfast
We brush our hair
We eat too much toast
I don't really care
Put on our flip-flops
And go to the beach
My mum always buys us
An ice cream each.

Lanna Grace Strachan (10)
Knightswood Primary School, Knightswood

Ghosts

The cold touch of Death
The shadowy figures
The thunderous voices
Screaming, 'Help us!'
Things that go bump
In the night
Trembling and shaking
With fear
Just a dream!

David Mowatt (9)
Knightswood Primary School, Knightswood

Fear

I fear there are venomous snakes
Under my bed
I fear that dead clowns
Will come and get me
I fear that zombies will
Eat my brains
And take me to the Underworld
I fear that if I shut my eyes
I will never open them again.

Scott Dundas (11)
Knightswood Primary School, Knightswood

I Can't Write A Poem

I can't write a poem
World War III has broken out
It's D-Day
I'm not in this class
I'm on the phone
Aliens are attacking me
There's a tornado coming
I was beaten up by a bear
I'm not doing it anyway
What? I've written a poem?
Yes! I did it!

Declan Kiely (10)
Knightswood Primary School, Knightswood

The Medal

Last seen April 1941
The medal was as silver as a diamond,
Now it is as black as night,
Covered in a layer of mud.

Covered in a layer of memories,
The memories as beautiful as the sun,
The memories as dark as night,
The memories that we can't remember
But the memories that he will never forget.

Lauren Ross (11)
Ladybank Primary School, Ladybank

The Gun

The moon like a medal hung in the sky,
The smell of smoke carried in the breeze.
The gun shoots,
Bang!

As long as a stick,
As wide as a needle,
As fast as lightning as he shoots
The bullet through the air.

He is a devil,
A terrible thing.
Why does he do it?
The deafening thing.

As loud as a siren ringing in your ear,
All that blood spilt with that one bullet,
It's as bad as a bomb flying through the air,
We all know it's over for the people under there.

Shot so many people,
But now it's all over,
It's lost in the dirt, mud oozing over.

Helen Forbes (10)
Ladybank Primary School, Ladybank

The Lost Helmet

Slightly bashed but all in one piece,
It could have saved a life.
That's what helmets are for, isn't it?
They shouldn't have had to wear them anyway.
They could have been teenagers or in their early twenties.

He shouted when the sirens started screaming
The wind started howling
The planes started bombing
Then it all went black.

He might have woken up
He might have stayed sleeping
Maybe that's how I got the helmet
When I was looking in the attic.
It was in the black leather trunk
As I fumbled with the lock I got
Butterflies in my tummy.

I lifted the lid and that's when I saw it.
Carefully I lifted it out of the trunk
It shone in the light
Then I saw the initials engraved into
The helmet
EJC, I knew who that was
It was my granddad,
Edward Joseph Cooke.

Robyn Sylvester (11)
Ladybank Primary School, Ladybank

The Locket

The moon was still and pale as the faces of the dead,
the bodies lay still in no-man's-land.
Wherever I look, blood follows my eyesight,
everything seems still, as if I were the only one left.

Hear the gunpowder under my feet as I tread,
hear a beautiful chime instead of a crunch.
Lift my feet with ease and care,
only to reveal a golden locket as dusty as a trench.

As I lean towards, the nearer I get, my heart pounds more,
pick it up with such care.
Wipe it down with my sleeve, only to reveal a heart,
click it open with gentleness, only to show his love.

An old photo, as clear as day,
black and white, shining like diamonds.
A merry tune playing its part, the writing speaks, 'Love you wherever you are'.

As I tilt my head slightly to the right,
to see the man that loved his locket with all his heart.
Only to lose all he had loved in a brutal way,
blade clutched to his side, to protect, only it didn't do its part.

Carry him all the way to a patch of earth,
to dig up a hole for him to stay.
Gently empty him into his new home,
put the locket on his died out heart, so his love will stay with him forever.

Abbey Given (11)
Ladybank Primary School, Ladybank

Public Tap

When I first got used I was as shiny as a star.
As clean as newly laundered clothes and as useful as a door.
Everyone needed me, everyone used me.
I was the cake at the wedding.
I felt amazing.
I had lots of different settings, warm and cold,
Even a handle that could turn 360 degrees.
My marvellously magnificent life was merry.
I wouldn't change it for anything,
Until, gradually *everyone* abandoned me.
I was alone, rusty, unwanted.
I sit here now isolated in the bacterial room.
All by myself.
Everyone hears my rusty cry, but nobody cares.
I get worse and worse each day.
I wish someone would love me . . . maybe one day.

Eilidh Warden (11)
Longforgan Primary School, Longforgan

The Computer

I am a computer that's in a haunted house.
My owner left me and abandoned me in this house
I feel as sad as rain now that nobody is using me.
I see nothing but darkness, cobwebs and my best friend, Bob the spider
Wait . . . I see people in the house!
They fling me into their truck as fast as lightning, then drive like a bull!
Wait . . . this is a garbage truck . . . why?
Suddenly, there's a blinding light!
I'm in computer heaven!
Goodbye, as I fly like a bird.

Ben Carroll (11)
Longforgan Primary School, Longforgan

The Rose

I see all the bonnie flowers.
All the flowers laughing, shouting and making fun of me.
I am so old I silently weep at night.
I am as red as a ribbon on a girl's dress.
Oh no, a lady chopped off my roots, taking me in a hot, sweaty car.
Where am I?
I am in a hospital.
I see this machine.
When I look over I see an old lady with a mask on her face.
I go back into the hot, sweaty car
I drive away, far away.
It's so hot, I feel my petals falling off.
I start to droop.
I'm slowly dying.
I'm in pain.
Nothing is going to help me.

Madeline Hayman (11)
Longforgan Primary School, Longforgan

Rocking Horse

I sit alone in a dusty attic,
No one wants me anymore.
I'm a rare antique but they didn't care.
The children played on me as if I was the last thing on Earth.
If I could talk I would plead, 'I only just need a lick of paint
And I'm as good as new.'
When I rocked back and forth it was as though I was free as a bird.
But now I'm, the last toy in the shop,
Unwanted and dusting away.
If I could cry, I would cry rivers.
Why do they not want me?
I wouldn't do any harm.
But I'm in an attic dusting away,
Unwanted but here to stay.

Erin Sandeman (12)
Longforgan Primary School, Longforgan

Teddy

I've been sitting here for days, where is she?
All I want is a cuddle!
She said I was as cute as a puppy.
What's wrong with me now?
I am a lonely watermelon sitting on a shelf, waiting for a home!
Nobody talks to me anymore.
Sadness fills me like water filling a cup!
If I could cry I would be crying a river.
I feel as though no one cares about me.
I'm the last biscuit in the biscuit tin.
Why does no one love me?
I just want a friend, someone to spend the long hours of the day with.
Hold on, there she is. What's she doing?
Bringing me down the long, winding stairs.
She brings me into the living room.
She has decorated the living room for a tea party and who is that?
It's a new person!
Maybe she can be my best friend.
Joy to the world, I've got a new best friend!
I'm as happy as a child opening a Christmas present.
I love my life and I am the luckiest person in the world!

Iona Vannet (11)
Longforgan Primary School, Longforgan

A Lonely Leaf

Only a month ago my friends and family surrounded me,
Now I am alone.
Discoloured and withered I cling on to the tree for dear life,
But today the winds are howling, clawing at my skin
And my grasp is weakening,
Slipping . . .
In a sudden gust of wind my home is gone and I'm tumbling down.
The ground is rushing up to meet me,
I brace for impact but it never comes,
I squeeze open my eyes, petrified of what I'll see,
Panning out beneath me is a colossal city twinkling in the afternoon sun,
The streets are flooded with traffic and people,
It's as busy as rush hour at a train station,
Suddenly I'm swirling downwards towards a city that's even bigger close up,
A tornado of twigs and litter envelop me,
The ground zooms up again but this time it doesn't stop,
In a blow that would shatter bones, I smack onto concrete.
If I could speak I'd be screaming in pain.
Down here it's filled with noise,
An angry lion roaring wildly.
I'm just recovering from the fall when I'm crushed.
It feels like I've been squished by a thousand boulders,
Then it's gone and I'm drifting towards grass.
When I look back, I realise I've landed on a road,
But nobody seems to care that I've been injured.
Nobody even seems to notice me.
Down here I'm powerless, useless,
As I am only a leaf and down here that means nothing.

Sophie Crowe (11)
Longforgan Primary School, Longforgan

Snowflake

I am a snowflake
And I am white
And I am very cold
And everybody likes playing with me
When I fall from the sky
Everything turns white
Then when I land on the ground
Everybody makes snowmen with me
When I fall from the sky
I don't fall straight
I fall diagonally
I am sad because when I fall
I make the roads slippery
Then people can't drive
When people play with me
I get hurt
I am lonely
Because I don't have any friends
Then when I fall on the roads
People have
To scrape me off the ground
When people drive
They can maybe get stuck sometimes
And they crash because of me
When I fall on the road
It becomes slippery.

Jonathan Nathan (12)
Longforgan Primary School, Longforgan

The Waiting Room Chair

I am the waiting room chair

I see a plump lady come in,
Snivelling, sniffing, sobbing,
She looks as downcast as a stray dog,
Please let her sit on me,
She picks my brother,
And stuffs a snotty tissue down his back.

I am the waiting room chair

Then I see a man come in,
Jumpy, jittery, joyful,
His face looks like the sun,
He looks more fun than the lady,
He heads towards me but then goes right,
He sits on the window seat.

I am the waiting room chair

A mum came in with three children,
Worn-out, worried, weak,
The mum sat on a chair next to the lady,
And nibbled her half-chewed nails,
The lady hands her a tissue,
Will anybody sit on me?

I am the waiting room chair

Then I see a nurse come in,
Confident, classy, clipboard,
She calls for a Miss Parker,
And the lady stands up,
'A bad thing has happened,'
Says the nurse, 'your husband has died.'

I am the waiting room chair

In comes a fat man,
Stamp, stomp, shout,
And sits on me.
I'm happy someone has put me in use,
But I hear a crack
And pain zips through my back like an F1 car.

I was the waiting room chair.

Rose Porteous (11)
Longforgan Primary School, Longforgan

The Leaf

I look around and all my friends and family are gone.
Right now I feel as lonely as though I'm the only person left on Earth.
I think today will be my last day as here the wind is sending shivers down my back which can only mean one thing.
I can feel myself getting weaker and weaker
As though someone is pushing me down.
Falling.
I thunder against the ground.
Around me an array of my kind.
People walk over, kick me, throw me up in the air like they just don't care.
If I had their legs I'd run far, far away from here.
If I had their eyes I'd cry a thousand tears
And if I had their arms I'd climb back up to where I belong.
Then I feel myself going higher and higher as I heat up instantly in their hands.
They're carrying me away, away from my kind
As I'm just a leaf.

Niamh Bethway (11)
Longforgan Primary School, Longforgan

Abandoned House

I live on the end of the road
Some people throw eggs at me
Bedrooms are in dust and spiders.
My wood keeps on falling around me,
My grass is dead.
Birds don't sit on me, that is very sad
People keep on kicking me.
All my windows are smashed out, my glass is everywhere
Dogs pee on me, that's not really nice.
All the trees beside me are dead
A bit of the grass is dead.
A bit of my roof has fallen off
People have never touched me for 100 years.
I wish I had legs to run away like people,
But it's not my fault I don't have legs.
I am like a hot dog with no ketchup,
But what is that? A car stopped in front of me.
That has never happened before, the child touched me.
Wow, I like that feeling, it is fantastic.
Now I will be happy forever.
I am so happy that my dreams have come true.

Dawid Lupina (11)
Longforgan Primary School, Longforgan

The Window

I was once cared for and cleaned
I was as clear as crystal
The owner left me open all my life
But now I see an old, abandoned warehouse
Forever I will rust and decay with grime and dirt
Spiders crawl all over me and leave cobwebs
Now children throw lumps of rock and stone at my friends and family
I hear the door open and a man comes in with a crowbar
He knocks my friends and family out of their frames
He comes over to me and pulls a cloth from his pocket and cleans me
Soon all I see is a factory making windows
Once again I am a crystal-clear window letting in light.

Sammy Simpson (11)
Longforgan Primary School, Longforgan

Titan Crane

As hard as iron, the gigantic Titan crane stands as tough as a tiger above me,
Reflecting off the green, murky water underneath me.
It is standing as still as a tree,
As the days go past.
Sadly, now it doesn't lift beautiful cruise liners,
But it is still as hard as an ox.

Jay Campbell (11)
Luss Primary School, Luss

The Titan Crane

As big as a building high in the sky.
Too high for you and I,
That is the Titan crane.
As scary as a snake when you look down.
Sometimes you barely hear a sound.
She waits for loads,
Looks up and down and all around.
That's the Titan crane.
Hooks as big as a horse,
Far too scary for me, of course,
That's the Titan crane.

Mollie Gear (10)
Luss Primary School, Luss

Titan Crane

I can see her shine reflecting off the water.
Her colour is as blue as the sky.
Slowly, her arm is creaking round,
When she's standing on the ground.

I can feel the hot rivets through my hand,
She's as powerful as the rain staring at me.
The ships lining up next to the quay,
The men working as busy as a bee!

Jenna Louise Campbell (11)
Luss Primary School, Luss

The Blue Mannie In My Wardrobe

Did you know there's a wee blue mannie in my wardrobe?
Nobody ever sees him but me.

He's sometimes my friend but sometimes not
And by the way, he has a dog called Dot with a giant blue spot.

He's a fan of Gok Wan and looks like Jackie Chan.
He sits down and watches TV, his favourite channel is CBBC.

At night he sits on my bed and plays with his ted.
He sings a song in his head, by the way his ted's called Fred.

When I'm not around and nowhere to be found,
He curls up on the ground and doesn't make a sound.

Now you know there's a blue mannie in my wardrobe.
Nobody sees him but me.

Libby Mae Sinclair (11)
Meigle Primary School, Meigle

Me And Jack

M y collie is black and white
E very day me and Jack play in the courtyard

A larms go when Jack jumps up
N ow we go for breakfast
D own the stairs as fast as lightning

J ack wags his tail and knocks Mum's cuppie flying
A tholl shouts, 'Leave my dog alone!'
C an I take Jack on a walk, Dad?
K neeling over to put his lead on, he tugs me out the door.

Catriona Isabella Convery (11)
Meigle Primary School, Meigle

The Boy's Toy

Never was there any boy
Who had such a mad and crazy toy.
It looped his mum and chased his sister
It gave his younger brother a blister.
It bit the dog and spilt the milk
It even ruined his mum's new silk

But one day his dad had to say
'Enough play for the weekdays'
He broke the toy and threw it in the bin
The boy thought it was a great sin.
His sister cheered, his brother whooped
His mother was glad she would never again be looped.

The boy however bought another
This time better than the other.
It rounded up his family in two
It shoved his younger brother down the loo
The boy lived with the toy in peace and harmony
Until one sad day the toy decided the boy would be history.

Lucy Scarlett (10)
Meigle Primary School, Meigle

Robert Burns

Rabbie was a guid lad,
The wee critter was sometimes sad,
He worked on the fairms
And had mony wee bairns,
He loved the banter
Like Tam O'Shanter,
And now he is a tartan hero.

Martin Donaldson (11)
Meigle Primary School, Meigle

My Cat, Dudley

My cat, Dudley, is a fluffy little cat,
He sits beside the fire and sleeps on the mat.

Most of the time he sleeps on my lap,
When he is bad Mum gives him a slap.

He widens his eyes like a little, white owl,
He gets up in a mood and gives a loud growl.

While he's grumpy, Mum puts out the food,
When he hears the rattle, he comes in a hungry mood.

He eats his food as happy as can be,
Then he sits down and snuggles into me!

Errin Barnett (11)
Meigle Primary School, Meigle

Pig

Once there was one pig on a farm
And he had a gun.
He tried to take over the farm,
But then the farmer brought out his axe
And soon there was none
And the farmer knew
What he was having for tea that night!
And all the animals laughed
With all their might.

Cameron McCord (10)
Meigle Primary School, Meigle

My Monsters

My monsters are big, fat and round,
They stamp and stamp all over the ground
One is red and one is blue
And one is sneezing on my shoe..
The yellow one eats kangaroo
And the green one smells like bamboo.
The blue one shot a cannonball
And knocked the pink one off the wall.

The purple one thinks he's great
And the orange one likes grapes.
The red one likes my flower bed
And the green one had a fuzzy head.
The yellow one made loads of cakes
Because the pink one had a break.
I love my monsters lots and lots
Because they have so many spots.

Jade Doig (10)
Meigle Primary School, Meigle

Cop And Dog

C ar siren wails loud,
O ver at the bank in town,
P eople pull over on the road,

A nd the police cars are going fast!
N ever before had the bank been on lockdown.
D anger at the gold safe.

D og is fast!
O ver at the bank so quick.
G uy the dog, saves the day!

He has the robber taken away!

Martin Melvin (10)
Meigle Primary School, Meigle

My Big Bro

Some people say my big bro is okay.
Some say he's lazy and he's kinda crazy.
Some say he's funny but not rich with money.
Some say he's annoying, I think he's kinda charming.
Some say he's nice, with blood as cold as ice.

My mum says he's smart, even smarter than 6th year, Bart.
He likes bangers and mash and has a bushy moustache.
He loves his black Lab, Abbi, even when she's kinda flabby.
Even though he goes to school late, my big bro is really great.

He has long hair and a wonky tooth and will never tell me the truth.
He has green eyes and is pretty tall,
I still remember when he put a hole in the wall!

He plays the keyboard 24/7, my mum said he was a gift from Heaven.
He really likes his Dorito dip and after it he lets one rip.
He plays his Xbox every day, that's why he never comes to play.

If you were wondering, he is a teen, and not very often he's pretty mean.
Some say my brother's yuck, but I'm just thinking, *go roll in the muck!*

I do stick up for him every once in a while
And when he makes me laugh, he brings a massive smile.

Megan Docherty (11)
Meigle Primary School, Meigle

The Moon

You shine like a big beam of light,
At midnight you light up the night.
Like a shining night-time sun,
Making the night look fun.

You are a circle of rocks floating in the air,
Like a big stone orbiting around us with care.
Made from a glowing shooting star,
To a shining moon afar.

Finlay Gilchrist (11)
Rhunahaorine Primary Schyool, Tayinloan

Sun

Closest star
It became
A glowing
Ball of gas
Bubbles
Boils hot
Sunspot
Gives
Energy
Heat
And
Light.

Malwina Kimak (7)
Rhunahaorine Primary Schyool, Tayinloan

The Zoo

As small as a button,
As tall as a tree,
All these animals are scared of just one thing,
Me!

Some are brutal, some are joyful
Some think they are king,
But fish live in water and birds live in trees,
And some just like to sing.

Racing rabbits running, kangaroos jumping,
Some are vicious and some are 'pawfect',
Some are cute, some are small,
And that's just the way they are.

Erin Doyle (9)
Robslee Primary School, Thornliebank

Mr Gareth Bale

Gareth Bale is fast and awesome,
As cool as a block of ice,
As awesome as a possum,
He is as thin as a grain of rice.

He is a wonderful wonder,
He is a goal magnet,
His shots are like thunder, *bang!*
And almost never misses target.

He is very quick,
He is so cool.
He can make the ball flick,
His house has a big pool.

Ben Cunningham (9)
Robslee Primary School, Thornliebank

The Summer Beach

The sand beneath your feet,
The shells a way under,
I always imagine there is no rain, lightning or thunder,
The fresh summer breeze,
The relaxing, hot sun, collecting shells in my bucket,
Oh, how it's so fun.
Water flowing upon my feet,
Waiting for me and her to meet.
The lovely salty ocean, I love how it flows,
In fact I love it so much,
I don't want to watch any TV programmes or shows.
Sometimes when the waves are high,
I feel like I can fly.
I remember one day I looked at the ocean,
It was blue, turquoise and green.
Sometimes I see seals, then it turns out it's just a dream.

Alyssa Neil (9)
Robslee Primary School, Thornliebank

Caterpillar

The caterpillar is 11 centimetres long
And is not very strong.
She's always bright as a daisy
And is never lazy.

She wants to have babies
And hopes they are ladies.
She is slimy and green
Hoping not to be seen.

The birds sing a sweet tune,
While she wraps up in a cocoon.
She is very happy, she starts to cry,
Because she's turned into a butterfly.

Yvonne McDonald (9)
St Bernard's Primary School, Shawhead

Egypt

Pharaohs like to dance around,
Just to the desert sound,
Pyramids are big and small,
Others are large and cool.

Encased in tombs full of dread,
Are where the mummies are laid to rest.
They worship gods with funny heads,
Tutankhamun was the best.

The Egyptians worshipped many gods,
Like Ra, god of sun.
They worshipped many more,
But Ra was the favourite one.

The River Nile runs so fast,
Just like Cleopatra's asp.
To the west of the Nile in the hills,
Is where you might find the Valley of the Kings.

Joshua McAuley (9)
St Bernard's Primary School, Shawhead

Pyramids

The pyramids are like enormous triangles
Made out of massive stones
The sun shines off it like a car window
It took 200 men to build it.

It took 20 years
Full of cheers
The tombs were built inside it
For dead people to live in.

They used ramps
To get up
And pulled boulders
That were tough.

Finally, the pyramids
Were done,
All the people were excited
And lay down in the sun.

Jay Wilkie (8)
St Bernard's Primary School, Shawhead

Wildlife

Ladybird so tiny and small
Caterpillar only two inches tall
Wild rabbits hop around
Little slug on the ground

Butterflies high in the sky
Trees so incredibly high
Seeds so snug in the ground
Flowers bloom all around.

Kara O'Neill (8)
St Bernard's Primary School, Shawhead

There's A Haggis In My Garden

There's a haggis in my garden,
He's been there for a while,
He's grumpy and he's smelly,
And I've never seen him smile.

He is so small and furry,
And wears a tartan hat,
I've seen him do the two step
With the neighbour's cat.

He steals stuff from my fridge each night,
It must be Irn-Bru,
My mum is always blaming me,
Because she hasn't got a clue.

I want to keep him in my house,
Because outside is always wet.
I wonder what my mum would say
If I asked to keep him as a pet.

Haleigh Hill (9)
St Bernard's Primary School, Shawhead

Cats

Small cats are very fun,
Huge big cats will make you run.
Big, black and mysterious through the night,
With eyes that glow like a big green light.

Big, stripy, fierce and fast,
Cats and dogs will give a blast.
Big, sharp, and fierce teeth,
This is good for cats because they love beef.

Small, cute, fluffy and black,
I hope I'll never be attacked.
Stripy, fierce, likes to eat little fish,
Big and small cats think they're delish.

Small, fierce and cute,
They like it when I play the flute.
Fast, fierce and small,
See them run down the hall.

Cailin-Marie Nisbet (9)
St Bernard's Primary School, Shawhead

I'm Practically Perfect

I'm practically perfect
Oh why can't you see?
It's just the way I am
It's easy to see.

I'm practically perfect
And ever so nice.
My mother and father
Say I'm precise.

I'm practically perfect
In so many ways,
That's what all my friends say.

I'm practically perfect
It's in my bones,
I snowballed and snowballed
Until it reached me alone.

I'm very spoilt and happy with that,
If I don't get my way,
I'm basically a brat.

I love being perfect,
It's the way I am,
Nobody can stop me,
Ha, ha, ha!

Lucy Provan (9)
St Bernard's Primary School, Shawhead

Divers Are Cool

When divers dive under the sea
There might be a diver called Lee.
Lee could find a shipwreck
Which maybe we could see.

He dives by day, not at night
He always knows he's right
Divers dive deep down
And explore the sea ground.

All kinds of treasures, all creatures he sees
Here in the quiet and peaceful sea
It gets deeper and deeper as he goes
He loves the water on his nose.

With an oxygen tank and a mask
He can stay underwater for hours
Learning about creatures
Taking photos to show to ours.

Calum Darren Moore (9)
St Bernard's Primary School, Shawhead

Flowers

F lowers waving in the air, pretty
L ovely smells like lavender so sweet-smelling
O n the summer days so good and so bright
W ow how pretty in the waving wind
E very day I pick some flowers for my mum so sick
R eally happy flowers in the vase so happy
S ome nice-smelling flowers which is a good present.

Hattie Lindhof (8)
St Mary's Episcopal Primary School, Dunblane

Wandering Mind

My mind wanders like a boat over the desolate sea,
Past cookies and LEGO, what a sailor I would be,
Or maybe a policeman chasing after crooks
But not a librarian with lots of books!

Sometimes my eyes wander to the clock,
The hands move so slowly, seems hours to the next tick-tock
The hands are like grannies racing round a track
As my mind wanders to small mice or a big fat rat.

When the teacher talks about spelling
My mind wonders about rebellion
When she talks about reading
My mind wanders back to dreaming.

Sometimes my mind wonders what I'm having for tea
I'm supposed to be writing a poem, wait . . . this is one!
Yippee!

Hamish Holmes (9)
St Mary's Episcopal Primary School, Dunblane

The Alphabet

The teachers make you learn it
It should never have been found
Most pupils hate to learn it
They want to bury it underground.

Keep it in a locked box
With guards all around
All the letters in there
Will never ever be found.

People might try to steal it
But never find the location
With guards all around it
The pupils would have a celebration
Because . . .
They will never have to learn the alphabet again.

Niall Baxter (9)
St Mary's Episcopal Primary School, Dunblane

My Pet Unicorn

'Your pet unicorn,' my sister said,
'Is a made-up animal,' when I was in bed
I don't believe her because when she's in bed
I take out my unicorn from behind the bedstead.

My pet unicorn is a baby
Unicorn with a white little horn coming
Out of her head and dear little wings
My pet unicorn is the prettiest of creatures
Well that's what I think!

When it is midnight, she comes out to play
I love to play tig and so does she
We sneak outside, she has a wee play
And so do I
Then we sneak back home to bed.

I always get up before anyone else
So I can feed my pet unicorn
Then I go up to my sister's bed
And wake her up!

Alex Taylor (8)
St Mary's Episcopal Primary School, Dunblane

Football

F ootball, you should try it, it is really easy
O ut the players go to play the match
O ff the post the ball went into the other player's feet
T ook the free kick and Ronaldo scored
B all went over the bar
A ll the crowd went mad
L ots of people went on the pitch when Real Madrid won
L ionel Messi was devastated that his team lost.

Charles O'Brien (9)
St Mary's Episcopal Primary School, Dunblane

The Massive Museum Of Awesomeness

At last the boy was running free
His wait was over, he was full of glee
The day he finally got to see
'The Massive Museum of Awesomeness'

Excited was he
To go and see
The paintings so grand,
The sculptures of sand,
The beauty of the land
And all that at
'The Massive Museum of Awesomeness'

Up the stairs avoiding falls,
Through the halls,
Down the passages in the walls

The boy, he really wants to see
The history
What he could be
Things that were lovely
At the best place in town
'The Massive Museum of Awesomeness'.

Alex Pearson (10)
St Mary's Episcopal Primary School, Dunblane

Rainbows

R is for the *r*ed of the rainbow,
A is for the *a*mazing aqua,
I is for the *i*ndigo like the dark night sky
N is for the *n*eon shine,
B is for the *b*right blue like the sea,
O is for the *o*range that stands out,
W is for the *w*hite in the pure clouds,
S is for the *s*uper colours of the rainbow.

Victoria Thomson (9)
St Mary's Episcopal Primary School, Dunblane

Maths

(Pupil)
'Maths, maths, I don't know how!
If you don't tell me I will get a big row.

Maths, maths, it's not very nice
Not to give me any advice.

Maths, maths, please help me,
Does one add one add one make three?

Maths, maths what does this mean?
Please tell me because I'm very keen.

Teacher, teacher, maths isn't helping!
Tell him please and I'll stop complaining.'

(Teacher)
'Maths, maths, if he doesn't know how
Just tell him so he won't get a row.

Maths, maths, it's not very nice
Not to give him any advice.

Maths, maths, you're annoying me!
Just tell him if the question makes three!

Maths, maths, tell him what it means,
Just tell him because he is very keen.

Bad boy, maths!'
'Sorry, Miss . . . '

Duncan Glen (9)
St Mary's Episcopal Primary School, Dunblane

One Day . . .

One day I went on a walk,
One day I had a big talk.
One day I went in my car,
One day I went to a bar.
One day I got a pet cat,
One day I went down and sat.
One day I went on a train,
One day I got a big stain.
One day I went on a bus,
One day I went in a fuss.
One day I woke up and said,
I'm staying right in my bed.

Rebecca Perry (8)
St Mary's Episcopal Primary School, Dunblane

I'm On the Road To Hampden

I'm on the road to Hampden to see my favourite team,
It's an important match, it's the last 16!
Dad got me a cup of fizzy Irn-Bru,
It's noisy through and through!
Samaras runs up, passes to Watt, it's a goal!
We all go hullabaloo, I nearly dropped my cup!
Red card to Barcelona, what luck.
The game carries on with lots of action
Horrendous fouls and a great strike.
Wait a minute it's a free kick, that's what I like.
Great save by Valdes, oh no it's one-all now!
135 minutes gone, still one-all, penalties now . . .

Archie MacKechnie (9)
St Mary's Episcopal Primary School, Dunblane

Once I Saw . . .

Timmy said: 'Once I saw a Jabberwocky
Playing hockey!

Once I saw a skeleton
That weighed a ton!

Once I saw a ghost
Eating Sunday roast!

Once I saw a zombie
Strolling in Abercrombie!

Once I saw a witch
Sitting in a ditch!

Once I saw a vampire
Invading an empire!'

Mum said: 'How gullible do you think I am?'
Timmy said: 'There's a sheep
That just went peep!'
Mum said: 'Where? Where?'

Euan Frize (9)
St Mary's Episcopal Primary School, Dunblane

Scotland

S cotland, what a beautiful country,
C ountryside all over the place,
O ver the seas we took America,
T he River Forth so big and mighty
L ots of battles waiting to happen,
A lot of mountains in this country,
N ice cities, such as Edinburgh, Aberdeen, Stirling and Dundee
D uncan the 1st got murdered by Macbeth in 1040.

Cory Gibson (9)
St Mary's Episcopal Primary School, Dunblane

A Triplet Of Musical Limericks

Melodies with their own tunes,
You could use wooden spoons,
Music is great
It's not up for debate
Though one thing you can't use is prunes.

I am now ready to go and play,
At the music concert today,
I am really excited
But my dog almost bited
My lucky dolly May.

I have now broken my hand,
Now I can't play in the band,
The band is ready
But I'm not steady
To play in the band called 'Sand'.

Laura Reid-Kay (9)
St Mary's Episcopal Primary School, Dunblane

Cardboard

C ardboard is amazing, you can do cool things with it
A tlantic salmon keeps you busy
R ubbish cardboard is to parents, they think it should go in the bin
D o they listen? What a waste of our voice and cardboard
B ut sometimes they win and it just ends up in the bin
O ut of our minds they think we were to say yes
A lthough it might be useful someday – maybe today
R ubbish cardboard, it isn't boring, we will play
D on't throw it away, please!

Keira Cant (9)
St Mary's Episcopal Primary School, Dunblane

Don't

(Inspired by Michael Rosen)

Don't hit your sister!
Don't ping your food at your sister!
Don't, don't, don't, don't
But do . . .
Help your sister tidy her room
Do eat your food properly
Do, do, do, do!

Órla Proctor (9)
St Mary's Episcopal Primary School, Dunblane

The Peace Wall

Belfast, where the peace wall stands,
Inside is a big hall where the Irish have land.

The two sides, Unionists and Catholics are separated by this wall,
But I don't want them to fight, I want peace and that is all.

The wall takes in visitors every day,
Who hope there will become peace in some way.

People, kids, tourists, everyone is signing the wall,
Hoping to bring peace to the Irish and all.

George Gornall (9)
St Mary's Episcopal Primary School, Dunblane

Buildings

B uildings are so very big
U nbreakable with strength
I nside it looks a miracle
L ong and strong is best
D own below all people stare
I n amazement everywhere
N othing can just top this sight
G reat big blocks in the sky
S pearing in the sky so high.

Sophie Perry (8)
St Mary's Episcopal Primary School, Dunblane

The Sky

T he sky is so peaceful and beautiful,
H earing the gentle breeze float past you,
E njoying watching the clouds swiftly moving past you.

S omeone always says to you the sky looks so brilliant,
K ites soaring above you,
Y ellow and orange sun comes out and shines on everyone.

Aron Curwen (9)
St Mary's Episcopal Primary School, Dunblane

The Blue Daffodil

The blue daffodil stood still on the sleepy, grassy hill.
Wishing if only there was something called the yellow pill.
Soon his only dream would come true.
His wish is that he wants to be not so very blue.
But to be a yellow daffodil just like all the other ones.
Many people see him and start to laugh.
And think his is so very, very daft.
But he just ignores them, though he finds it hard.
But the good thing about being blue is you get a birthday card!

Gabriella Toop (8)
St Mary's Episcopal Primary School, Dunblane

Don't . . .

(Inspired by Michael Rosen)

Don't eat with your mouth open
Don't breathe too loud
Don't sit on Dad's chair
Don't change the clock round
Don't watch too much TV
Don't do these when Dad's at home

But do use your chair
Do read a lot
Do play with your friends
Do these when Dad's at home
Do these a lot!

Sam Carr (9)
St Mary's Episcopal Primary School, Dunblane

Rugby

Crash! Boom!
There goes Richie Gray
Try by Rickie Gray
Laidlaw let it fly!

Ardán Proctor (8)
St Mary's Episcopal Primary School, Dunblane

Weekend!

W eekends are fun!
E xciting weekends
E xtraordinary weekends
K nowing all that I have, I get bored.
E ducated or not, I need a break.
N eglected I feel because I've got no one to play with.
D ark or not, I love playing outside

Amie Marshall (10)
St Ninian's Episopal Primary School, Perth

Snow White

She has eyes of pure gold,
And lashes like a lion's mane,
Thick and gorgeous,
No need for shame.

Eyelids of lavender,
Eyebrows of a daisy's stem,
Ink-black and beautiful,
Curved right to the end.

Teeth like white shiny snow,
And lips as red as a rose
Perfectly rounded,
Well as far as I know.

A figure of beauty,
And papery-white skin,
With cheeks like prink fuchsias
She has a beautiful grin.

Hair as dark as coal,
And a red, red hair bow,
A way with little animals
From rabbits to crows.

Snow White is just a little girl
Who is the most beautiful in all the world,
According to the mirror on the wall,
She's the fairest of them all!

Abbie Maclaughlan (11)
St Ninian's Episopal Primary School, Perth

The Hobbit

There was a man from the shire,
That gold wasn't his desire,
He fled from his hill,
And went past the mill,
To kill a dragon with fire!

He met a man like a bear,
And that he couldn't bear,
He saw some trolls,
And had many roles,
And goblins he had to tear!

He went to the last homely house,
When leaving he felt like a mouse,
He went through a wood
And was in a bad mood,
And the spiders there were like louse!

He found a mystical ring,
That he also had to win,
He went through some mines,
And got lost many times,
And got armour stronger than tin!

Thomas Law (10)
St Ninian's Episopal Primary School, Perth

Poor Old Craig

There was an old man called Craig,
Who never got rid of the plague,
One day he fell over and died,
His wife and children cried,
And that was the end of old Craig.

Ailsa Gourlay (11)
St Ninian's Episopal Primary School, Perth

The Nether

Let's go mining with my trusty pick,
It's a claustrophobic experience so don't be sick.
I found some obsidian, over here!
It looks so black, like the eye of a deer.

Let's build a portal to the Nether,
I guess it's just for the better.
I'm not very fond of the Endermen,
So the End is not the place for me then.

I think of the Nether as a very nice place,
Whoops! Before I go I'd better tie my shoelace.
I enter the portal, out the other side I come,
I see a pigman staring at me, his face so glum.

The lava is flowing all around me,
No trees, no animals – not even a bee!
I see a ghast, high up in the sky,
I aim my bow, shoot my arrows up high.

I see a burning blaze,
Far away in the haze.
A magma block over there!
Cosy in its Nether fort lair.

The blaze seems to be getter bleaker and bleaker,
No wait, it's coming nearer and nearer!
We must go now, before it's too late.
Let's run! Let's run! We must make haste!

I thought of the Nether as a very nice place,
(How wrong I was).
Now I know the Nether is *not* a nice place!

Euan Hutchison (10)
St Ninian's Episopal Primary School, Perth

Tim

There once was a boy named Tim,
There is no other boy like him,
He once read a book.
That his half-sister took,
And his half-sister is called Kim.

Kim thinks Tim is so ignorant,
She always gives him just a little hint,
Kim's still got that book,
That one of Tim's she took,
And Tim thinks Kim is not important!

Rhiannon Dick (10)
St Ninian's Episopal Primary School, Perth

Holidays

H ives full of buzzing bees
O ceans with roaring waves
L ie-ins
I n the hotel
D igging in the sand
A ll-you-can-eat buffet
Y ellow shining sun
S ailing on a boat.

Peter Godfrey-McKay (11)
St Ninian's Episopal Primary School, Perth

The Wind

The wind is a cold long breeze,
When I feel it I shiver my knees.
The wind can spread about the room,
It can also lead you to your doom.

The wind is fierce and cold,
You can't see it but it's big and bold.
Every day when I'm walking down the street,
I can feel it even on my feet.

The wind, it's big and powerful,
But you might just think that it's dull.
You really need to get to know it
Just maybe a little bit.

Jenna Holden (10)
St Ninian's Episopal Primary School, Perth

Summer

S ummer is really hot and sunny!
U nder the sea or going swimming!
M y birthday is usually hot and sunny!
M ight go to the beach!
E xciting!
R eally hot!

Niamh Moran (10)
St Ninian's Episopal Primary School, Perth

A Poem About Food

Oh how you are bad and good
At some point you think of food
When you hear your belly rumbling
You know you need to give it something
When you need to treat your tum
You know it won't do good to your bum
A chocolate bar, a packet of crisps
Oh what do you do?
You go for a run to think it all over
Be careful that you don't fall over
You need to lose weight because you
Are six pounds over
I haven't weighed myself in a while . . .
I shall get the scales
I get on with one foot, then the other
Oh my gosh I am six pounds under!
Nine stone and five foot five tall
I guess I deserve a cake after all.

Courtney Kinnaird (11)
St Ninian's Episopal Primary School, Perth

School

School is fun as can be
Everyone likes it, even me.

Wake up, get dressed
Go to school, it is the best.

School is fun and
Everyone likes me.

3 o'clock is the best part of the day
When I get home I go outside and play.

Cody Gunn (10)
South Lodge Primary School, Invergordon

In The Dark And Ancient Graveyard

In the dark and ancient graveyard,
Zombies rise up from the grave.
They meet each other to dance,
Soon they are twirling in a trance.
When dawn is about to crack,
The zombies sip back.
Back to the grave until the next midnight dance.

Calvin Russell (10)
South Lodge Primary School, Invergordon

Winter

I love winter by the log fire
And the beautiful snow that I desire.
Hat and scarf on you go
To keep me warm from the snow,

The sledge goes down the snowy hill
Sledging takes a bit of skill.
I love to make a snowman
Can it move? Yes it can.

In winter there are celebrations
And money for charity donations,
Everywhere there is snow
Everywhere that it blows.

Presents under the Christmas tree
Oh look that one's for me.
A time to say thanks for what I got
To say thanks that they never forgot.

Sometimes the snow can be a pain
Up my chimney, down the lane
Down on my head falls a snowflake,
It comes down with a wee shake.

The snow falls to the ground
Silently without a sound.

Jean Anderson (11)
South Lodge Primary School, Invergordon

My Dog Max

My dog Max
Is brown and white
My dog Max
Just loves to bite anything
That's edible unless it's a vegetable.

He will chew the stuffing in his bed
Or dislocate his teddy's head
He will inhale the dog food in his dishes
When he is eating he is very vicious
Even though he loves to eat,
My dog Max is very sweet.

My dog Max is sometimes crazy
His nickname is the Great Destroyer
He licks and chews everything in sight
He won't bite, but beware of his might.

Dylan Thorpe (10)
South Lodge Primary School, Invergordon

Winter

On that winter's day the ground
Was so cold as it lay.

The stones were so cold as they lay
They were still as night.

On that cold winter's night
The raindrops were still.

No one could move a muscle or two.

It was all silent as night
On that cold winter's night.

Denver Mackenzie (11)
South Lodge Primary School, Invergordon

Fear

Fear is a horrible thing
Fear makes me jump out of my skin
Fear is a lonely place
Just like down at the war base
Fear gives you a shake
Goosebumps pop up and awake
It is frightening, lonely
And you're in a small, cold alleyway.

Leoni Widdows (10)
South Lodge Primary School, Invergordon

Fly

I wonder what it's like to fly
I wonder what it's like to whizz into the sky.
A pair of wings pop out of my back
I set off with a flap.
I shoot up into the air
My hair is going everywhere.
I spin and whizz in the sky
Above everything that can fly.
Everyone in the town looks up at me
I could just see the faces of my family.
I looked down, I almost fell
Now I really don't feel well.
I try to pull down but it goes wrong
I'm falling down forever long.
I close my eyes, I tell a lie
Now I really don't want to fly.

Eilidh Gunn (10)
South Lodge Primary School, Invergordon

Manchester United

Manchester United champions 19 times
I don't know how so I just say wow!

Players as good as can be
They won't let past a busy bee

There's Rooney, there's Welbeck
Better than me

The Manchester rival, Man City United
Oh my gosh I'm so excited

When they score a goal
The crowd go 'Oh!'

The strip, red and white
There will always be a fight

Defenders as good as can be
They won't let past a busy bee.

Luke Widdows (10)
South Lodge Primary School, Invergordon

My Hamster

My hamster is very fat
She is nearly half the size of a cat
The cage is small and that is it
I think I need to stretch it a bit.

She climbs fast up the wall
So make sure she doesn't fall
She is brown, grey, white and black
If she was a boy I would call her Jack.

All the time she runs down the stairs
Climbs up the rope and onto the chairs
Her cage is so tall she climbs up the bars
I think she is climbing a bit too far.

Anusha Williamson (10)
South Lodge Primary School, Invergordon

The Footballer

The footballer is a star
He has a fancy car
He makes the ball rise
He always gets a golden prize
He makes the stadium very busy
The manager is very dizzy
The weather is mild
The crowd go wild
They go to get a football top
And they're all out of stock
They go back in a hurry
So they don't miss the curry.

Mikey Thorpe (10)
South Lodge Primary School, Invergordon

Spain

Phew, it's hot in Spain,
Just got off the plane.
Suitcases whizzing round,
Can't wait till mine is found.

Hot sun rising in the sky,
Sun lotion on, don't want to fry.
No clouds to be seen,
Think I need an ice cream.

Smooth sand slides through hands,
Running and jumping in the sand.
Sandcastles tall and small,
Having fun with a beach ball.

Now it's time for a swim,
In the seas all shimmering,
With its waves all sparkly and blue,
So much fun, so much to do.

Lex Whittenham (11)
South Lodge Primary School, Invergordon

My Family

My family is very silly
But I like my cousin Billy
He is very mad
But sometimes he is bad
When my mum is evil
I go on Binwevil
When my mum is good
I think I should cut some wood
My dad is cool
He likes a bit of pool.

Weronika Firkowska (10)
South Lodge Primary School, Invergordon

My Sister

My sister is like an angel in the sky.
She makes me want to fly
Up high away in the clouds,
She makes me want to scream out loud.

She makes me want to dance and sing all day long.
She is like a singing song.
She thinks I'm just a little girl,
But I think I'm a little pearl.

She gives me sweets if I'm good,
But only if she's in a good mood.
I wish she was always so jolly,
So I could get more chocolate lollies.

Kathryn Fraser (10)
South Lodge Primary School, Invergordon

Music

Music, music everywhere.
It's great to sing, it's great to share.

I lose myself in a trance,
I forget inhibitions and I just dance.

Heavy metal, shake it about
Scream and jump, dance and shout.

Pink Floyd, a thoughtful band
I like to listen, still is my hand.

Alternative music is quite different
To listen you have to pay your rent.

I think rock music is quite brilliant
It's one of my favourites, it helps me try when I think I can't.

Music is one of my favourite things
It gives me hope and my heart sings

One day I will play in a band
My folks will be proud as I sing and stand.

Corey Macleod (10)
South Lodge Primary School, Invergordon

Fear

Fear is cold like a cold dark night.
Fear is sadness and definitely badness.
Fear is like being stuck in a small cardboard box
Covered all over with chickenpox.
Ring, ring I answer my phone
I don't know who it is
So with fear and in trepidation I call home.
I look out my window and guess who it is?
A zombie gravedigger in the mist.

Jamie Atcheson (10)
South Lodge Primary School, Invergordon

The Storm

The storm blowing like a howling wolf;
Frightened, screaming, fearful of night.

The sounds crashing against the peace
Like a sea crashing against the rocks.

Devastation all around
Morning makes a frightening frown.

We smell fear of scared people
Pressure is pounding in their hearts.

At last it has gone and we shout *hooray!*
Me and my friends go out to play.

Reece Hunter (10)
South Lodge Primary School, Invergordon

Callanish Stones

Callanish Stones standing for eternity
Callanish Stones as rough as a cat's tongue
Callanish Stones reaching for the sky
Callanish Stones casting a black shadow

Tourists stumbling over rabbit holes
Tourists taking photos of ancient monoliths
Tourists hiking to the spot
Tourists walking through a puzzling maze

Callanish Stones towering over lands
Callanish Stones battered by gusting gales
Callanish Stones growling, protesting
Callanish Stones waiting for long summer nights.

Cameron Baird (10)
Stornoway Primary School, Stornoway

Callanish Stones Fantasy Poem

Callanish Stones are swiftly walking past me
Swaying in the breeze!
During the night they come alive and
Start shouting at me!
As they chase me
I run as fast as I can
Petrifying stones brushing against the grass.
Grass as spikey as a thorn.

Pretending that they're not alive
Then jumping out and shouting
'I am coming to get you!'
Spooking me every night.
Beautiful in daylight but
Creeping me out at night
As I leave, they peer over me
Trying to give me nightmares
It doesn't work

Grass is so elegant and bright.
Stones are peering over me.
When it is windy
And the grass comes out of the ground,
Little pinches, falling up from the ground
They float in the air so lightly.
Birds calling as they fly past
Remind me of the Callanish Stones.
As the gleaming sun goes down
The stones are so delighted

Peacefully I walk past the fascinating stones
Eating a delicious ice-cream cone
Juicy, green grass blowing away with the wind
Could it even blow the stones down?

Samantha Macaulay (10)
Stornoway Primary School, Stornoway

Darkness Descends

Sparkling, soundless sea
Rolling under the smiling sky
Golden, glittering sand, hissing
Watched by the gazing sun

Soundlessly, the gentle sea
Closes its arms around the whispering sand
A curled up polar bear of cloud
Inhaling the salt of the mighty sea

Rolling green hills
To where the scarlet sun descends
Taking away all form of light
Playful waves still roll

Misty moon appears, illuminating
Sweeping the darkness out of the sky
Wilder waves start to roar
No longer the waves are playing.

Matthew Hanlon (10)
Stornoway Primary School, Stornoway

Beautiful Coll Beach

Soft, shimmering sand
Sinking under my feet
Blinding hot fiery sun
Smiling at me

Children laughing happily
Building towering sandcastles
Gentle, whispering winds
Racing tide approaches

A silent audience of gulls
Diving for fish
Colourful shells
Beautiful sounds of the Atlantic.

Caitlin Macaulay (10)
Stornoway Primary School, Stornoway

Lews Castle

Yellow, shimmering sun dances
Repeatedly the rain batters me
But I will continue to watch
Always, I will stand to attention

I will never stop guarding
Silently I stare down at the castle grounds
I will continue to stay strong
Sturdy I stand, I will not crumble

My walls now abandoned
Watching calm, starry nights and tremendous storms
I will continue to be part of history
I will never leave my foundations

Tourists admire my exterior
My towers reach up the heavens
I will continue to stand proudly
Not even the greatest can make me fall

My enemies are still not gone
Damaged yes, but repaired to best
I will continue to rule
My noble past lives on.

Ross Bain (10)
Stornoway Primary School, Stornoway

Legends Of Lewis

Wherever I look, I constantly see
Avenues of luminous rocks
They're staring at me
Big and black
Tall and stately

Wherever I look, I constantly see
Green grass growing
Rustling in the breeze
Shadows twist, shadows turn
Scorching sun tries to burn

Wherever I look, I constantly see
White clouds fleeing
White clouds racing
Vibrant birds perched up high
Singing their sweet morning song

Wherever I look, I constantly see
Ancient black rocks of history
Haunting stories
Blissful memories
Towering monoliths protecting the land

Wherever I look, I constantly see
Mesmerised tourists
Looking in awe
Admiring the beauty
As the stones hold everyone safely within their hands.

Dylan Glover (10)
Stornoway Primary School, Stornoway

The Beach

Yellow sand shimmering in the sun
Salt water splashing
Cliffs peering over me

River flowing to a foamy sea
Thick clouds are like marshmallows
Soft sand hissing

Rocks staring at me
Caves echoing the crashing waves
Bright sun smiling at me

Sea roaring at me
Dark rocks glaring at me
Yellow sand burning my feet.

Stewart Macleod (10)
Stornoway Primary School, Stornoway

Thrashing Seas

Dark skies roaring
Fearsome lightning hits the ground
Thrashing waves overpowering sandy beaches
Thunderous clouds cover blue skies
Violent seas growling

Sand twisting like tornadoes
Shimmering sand spraying
A storm now on the beach
Atlantic waves crashing against the towering cliffs
Ocean's fury finally unleashed.

Katryn Morrison-MacDonald (10)
Stornoway Primary School, Stornoway

Roaring Atlantic Ocean

Atlantic sea crashing
Against sharp rocks
Long, thin grass,
Brushing long, bare legs
Wild flowers stretching
Towards the red hot smiling sun

Jagged cliffs race
Ahead of me
Jagged cliffs stroll
Behind me
Birds glide
Through whistling winds

Bright boats race
Through roaring seas
Beaming lighthouse, towering
Towards stormy skies
Blinking in the darkness
Guiding boats to safety

Katie Hall (10)
Stornoway Primary School, Stornoway

War Memorial

Stornoway War Memorial towers over me
Roaring, howling wind
Trembling trees, racing leaves
Stornoway War Memorial
A mighty guard

Haunting eyes stare
Reminding us of lost souls
Telling tragic stories
Tearful tear sink into the ground
Heartbreaking memories

Daniel Macdonald (10)
Stornoway Primary School, Stornoway

War Memorial

Pearly ice crackling
Beneath my feet
Crunching
Stornoway War Memorial watching over me
Darkness descends on Lewis
Wind whistling
Stars twinkling

Standing still
Reaching towards the galaxy
To the twinkling stars
Staring at me
Smiling under the evening glow
Stornoway War Memorial
Dreaming

Haunting memories revealed
Crying for lost soldiers
Who never came back home
Lost sweethearts
Lost souls
Lost sons
Lost, but never forgotten

Anna Macaulay (10)
Stornoway Primary School, Stornoway

Callanish Stones

Towering over me, frightening me
The lofty stones trap me in their shadow
Stopping me in my tracks
At first sight, they startle me
Impossible to conquer
Historical Callanish Stones.

Ben Robinson (10)
Stornoway Primary School, Stornoway

War Memorial

High up on the hill
Peering over the town
Groaning in the rain
Wind howling around

Scottish flag flapping proudly
An eruption of precious poppy wreaths
Windows shattering, lightning flashing
A storm coming from murky seas

Rain pounding on the ground
Green grass turning to squelchy mud
Sitting on the hill for ninety years
Crying out for long lost soldiers

Standing proud for all to see
Allowing soldiers to share memories
Illuminating the dark night sky
Standing for all eternity.

James Macleod (10)
Stornoway Primary School, Stornoway

Coll Beach

Stormy skies moaning
Black clouds racing
Rough seas roaring
Desperate to attack a boat
Sand blowing
One direction

Elegant seagulls hovering
Dark caves surrendering
To the mighty, angry sea
Heavy hailstones falling
Helpless crabs
Clinging to home.

Bethany Davidson (10)
Stornoway Primary School, Stornoway

Deadly Beasts of Holm

Colossal waves boom
Seething seas surround Lewis
Dark clouds race over the grey sky
Tentatively, I open the gates
Iolaire Memorial awaits

Towering over me
I walk up the long, winding path
Big, bold writing calls me
A reminder of those who died
Tragedy on the island

I stand there, lost in thought
Staring at the deadly Beasts of Holm
Standing, freezing cold
Darkness descends
I taste the cold bitterness of loss

Heartache for heroes, who
Survived war, but
Now lost souls
So near to home
Sorrow, suffering for the island.

Kelly Cameron (10)
Stornoway Primary School, Stornoway

Creepy Callanish Stones

A sunny summer's day
Stones staring
Staring at me
Fiery sun smiling
Disappearing into the still seas

I'm lonely
But not alone
For the stones stand by my side
Gigantic, gloomy
Glaring at me

Luminous moon, shining
Midnight owls, hooting
Creepy black shadows surrounding
Blood-curdling ghosts scaring my soul
In darkness

Creeping up on me
Chasing after me
Shouting
Grabbing
Towering.

Rosie Sullivan (10)
Stornoway Primary School, Stornoway

Beautiful Beach

Beautiful buckets, scarlet spades
Shining sea and shimmering sand collide

Soft sand slowly sinks under me
Tickling my bare feet
Swish, the sea hugs the sand

A gentle wind, quietly whispers in my ear
Bright sun, stares at me cheerfully
Quickly, calm sea follows me
It has to run to keep up

Children on the pier, ready to jump
Splash!
Fun in sparkling seas
Swimming back to shore
Laughing and shouting
Waves calling for happy children.

Annabel Campbell (10)
Stornoway Primary School, Stornoway

The Forest Of Autumn Trees

The leaves are falling thickly and the wind is blowing lightly
as the deer run through the wood.

Then suddenly they stopped without a sound in a clearing
surrounded by falling leaves of crimson, gold and orange.

It is very quiet as the deer totter round and round
as sycamore seeds helicopter to the ground.

Squirrels scurry along the branches
holding their nuts tightly in their hands.

Autumn is coming!

Meg Leaver (7)
Teanassie Primary School, Kilmorack

Ice Cream

Ice cream, ice cream you're cold like the North Pole.
When the ice cream is melting it's time for testing.
Ice cream, all their flavours of ice cream,
Strawberry, mint choc chip, chocolate and vanilla.

Scott Beaton (9)
Teanassie Primary School, Kilmorack

Skating

People skate, scratching over lumps.
Figure skaters do terrific jumps.
All colours from black to blue swiftly glide.
Many argue, laugh and collide.
Under feet curl and curl.
Over bodies whirl and whirl.
Beginners can easily fall.
The tall stand over all.
Some people wear glitter.
Others are as fast as a flicker.
Marks on the ice fade away.
'Look what I can do,' they say.
People wrap up from the cold.
Skates that cannot slide are old.
I feel like I am grating.
I am happy when I am skating.

Christy Macpherson (9)
Teanassie Primary School, Kilmorack

The Poem Of Bill

When I was young
I had a very long tongue.
I could touch the sky.
I grew so tall
I would always fall
And soon I could touch the moon.

James Madden (7)
Teanassie Primary School, Kilmorack

Colourful Autumn

Lovely trees everywhere when it's autumn
All of the trees twirl crimson, gold and orange on the leaves.
The leaves are always wonderful at autumn.
Everyone dances to the music.
At night the leaves are dancing to the beat.
The trees are shining, leaves are floating.
There is a place where it's autumn.
The sound is beautiful.
Now it's going to be wintertime again.

Tamara Gill (7)
Teanassie Primary School, Kilmorack

Flowers

Pretty flowers blowing in the wind.
The bees take nectar from the flowers
Because they have secret powers
The rainbow behind the meadows
Birds looping round the rainbows.

Anna Owen (7)
Teanassie Primary School, Kilmorack

Kites

Night, not time for kites
All the stars are shining
All over the big black night
Everyone is in their beds
All ready for Firework Night.
Shooting rocket doing its job.

Angus Mearns (7)
Teanassie Primary School, Kilmorack

Evacuee Poem

Mother says it's not safe here anymore
I am going to have to go somewhere I have never been before
A tear dropped from my mother's face
'I hope you won't forget me when I leave without a trace.'
'Come on now son you will be late for your train,
You know I'm already suffering enough pain.'
I get on the train and say goodbye,
Looking sadly at my mother who begins to cry.
I whisper to myself, 'It will be all right!'
As I'm staring at the land Hitler plans to bomb tonight.
The train finally stops, the doors crash open
I see the man I'm going to be staying with,
He looks nick I'm hoping
I stare at him strangely with a pout,
'Are you Ben Phillips?' he shouts.
'Yes, that's me, just simple old Ben.'
'It's just your tag is badly written, must've been
a bad pen.'
I get to the house, it looks cosy and warm
And think about London it will be a raging swarm
'Are you hungry?' the man asks me.
'No sir I'm fine, I've already h ad my tea.'
'I've got some work that needs done
So you go out and have some fun.'
'Alright sir I'll do just that, let me go in and I'll
fetch my hat.'
I ran to my room and put my gas mask on the cabinet,
Saw my hat and quickly nabbed it.
The air smelt nice, the paths were clean
And all the people were the very opposite of mean
I went back home, dinner was on the table
Could I eat it? I was able.
'Eat that up and then it's bedtime.'
'OK sir that sounds just fine.'
I scoffed my tea like a king

I went upstairs to get into bed
With a lovely picture of Mother in my head.
I shut my eyes and began to snore
With lovely thought that my new home
Was loved to the core.

Lois Barr
Tweedbaml Primary School, Tweedbank

Snow Time

Soft snowballs shooting in the sky
Skiers skiing from the slippery hill
Snowflakes falling from the sky.
Snow is fun to play with.
Sparkly ice shimmers in the sun.
Snowmen get made and they are fun to play with.

Blake McBride (7)
Valley Primary School Kirkcaldy

Sparkling Snow

Sparkling snow lying on the ground in the sun
Snowballs in the air and melting.
Snowman has a scarf and gloves.
Squishy and squashy snow in the garden.
Sledge going down the slidey and icy hill.

Chloe Laing (7)
Valley Primary School Kirkcaldy

YOUNG WRITERS INFORMATION

We hope you have enjoyed reading this book - and that you will continue to enjoy it in the coming years.

If you like reading and writing poetry drop us a line, or give us a call, and we'll send you a free information pack.

Alternatively if you would like to order further copies of this book or any of our other titles, then please give us a call or log onto our website at www.youngwriters.co.uk

Young Writers Information
Remus House
Coltsfoot Drive
Peterborough
PE2 9BF
(01733) 890066